Within the intricate details of a mandala lies the seeker's journey, where art becomes a pathway to self-discovery and a reflection of the innermost soul.

This book is dedicated to you.

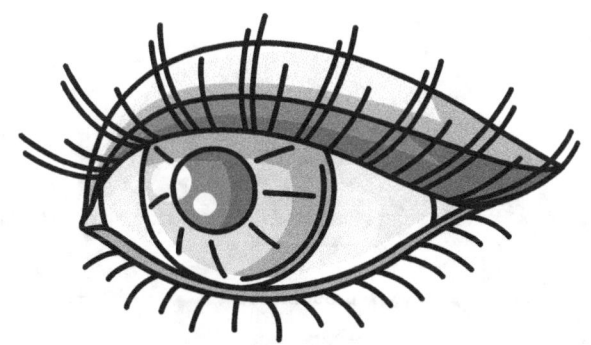

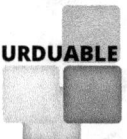

URDUABLE

www.urduable.com

101 MANDALA WITH PROMPTS | BY ABBY RAM |

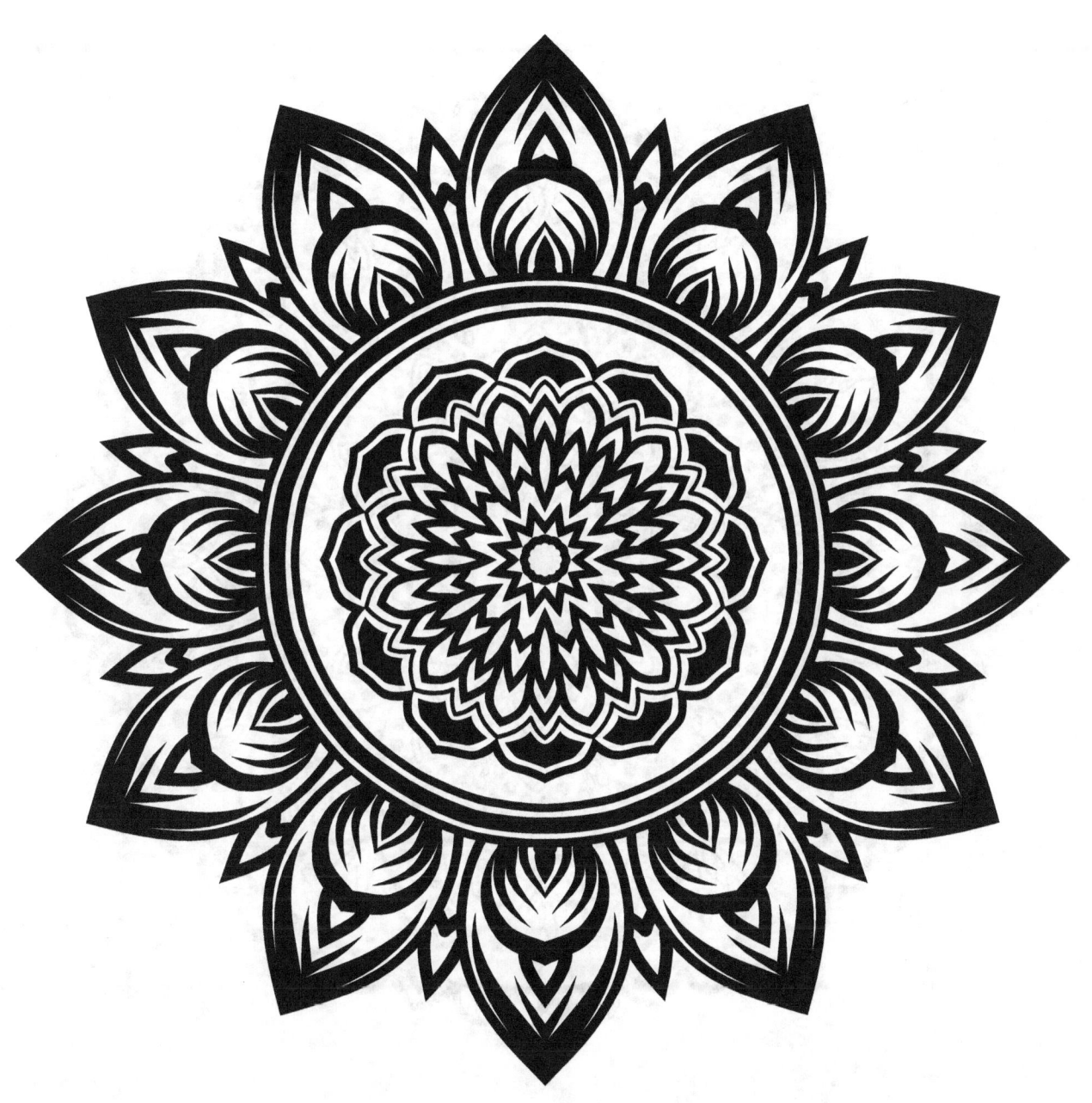

It's about a night in Tokyo with its glamorous rhythm and essence. Make it neon, glitzy and stylish.

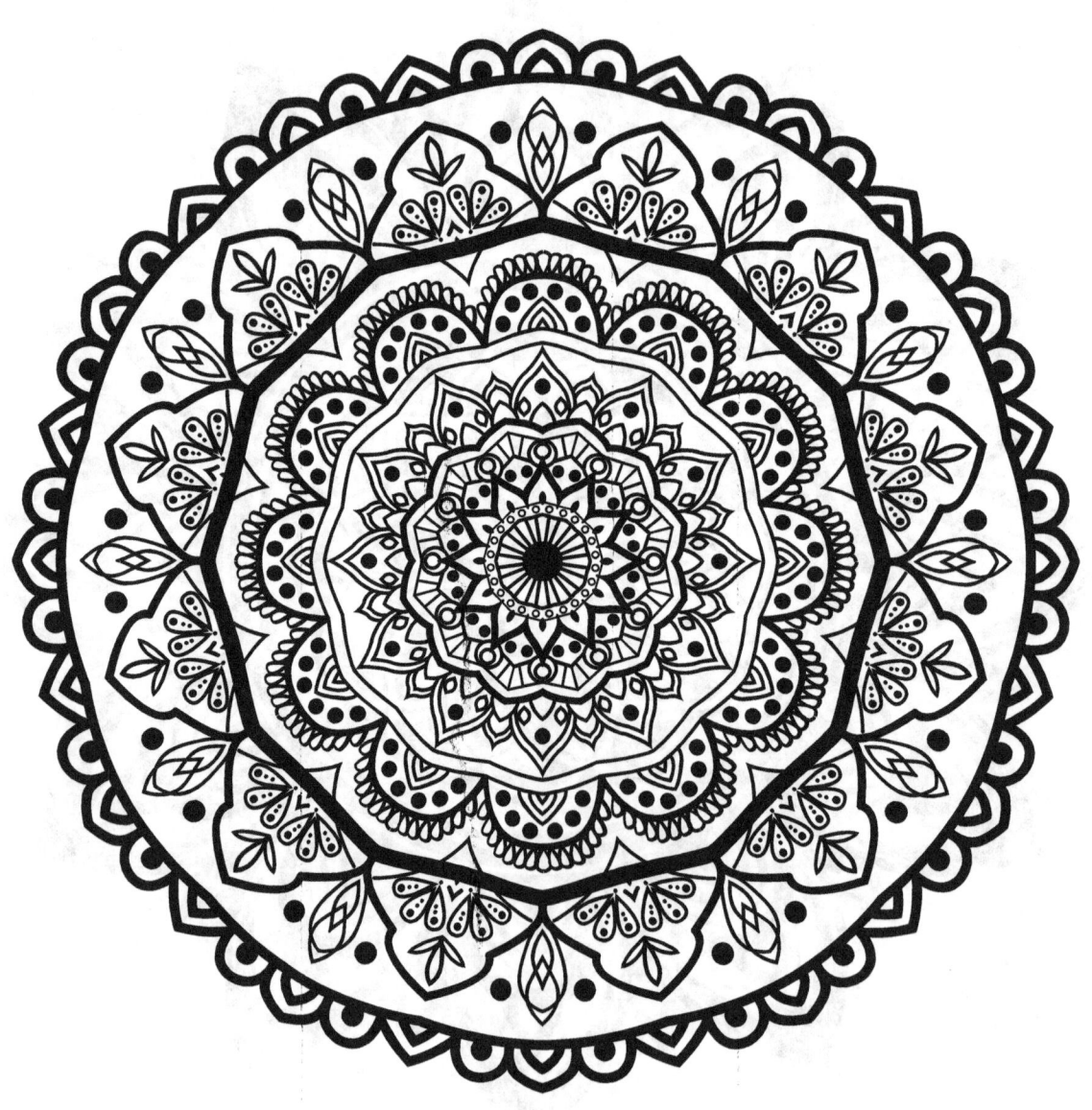

Think of a garden on a bright day. The combination of white, cream, pale blue and shades of green creates a soft, fresh event atmosphere.

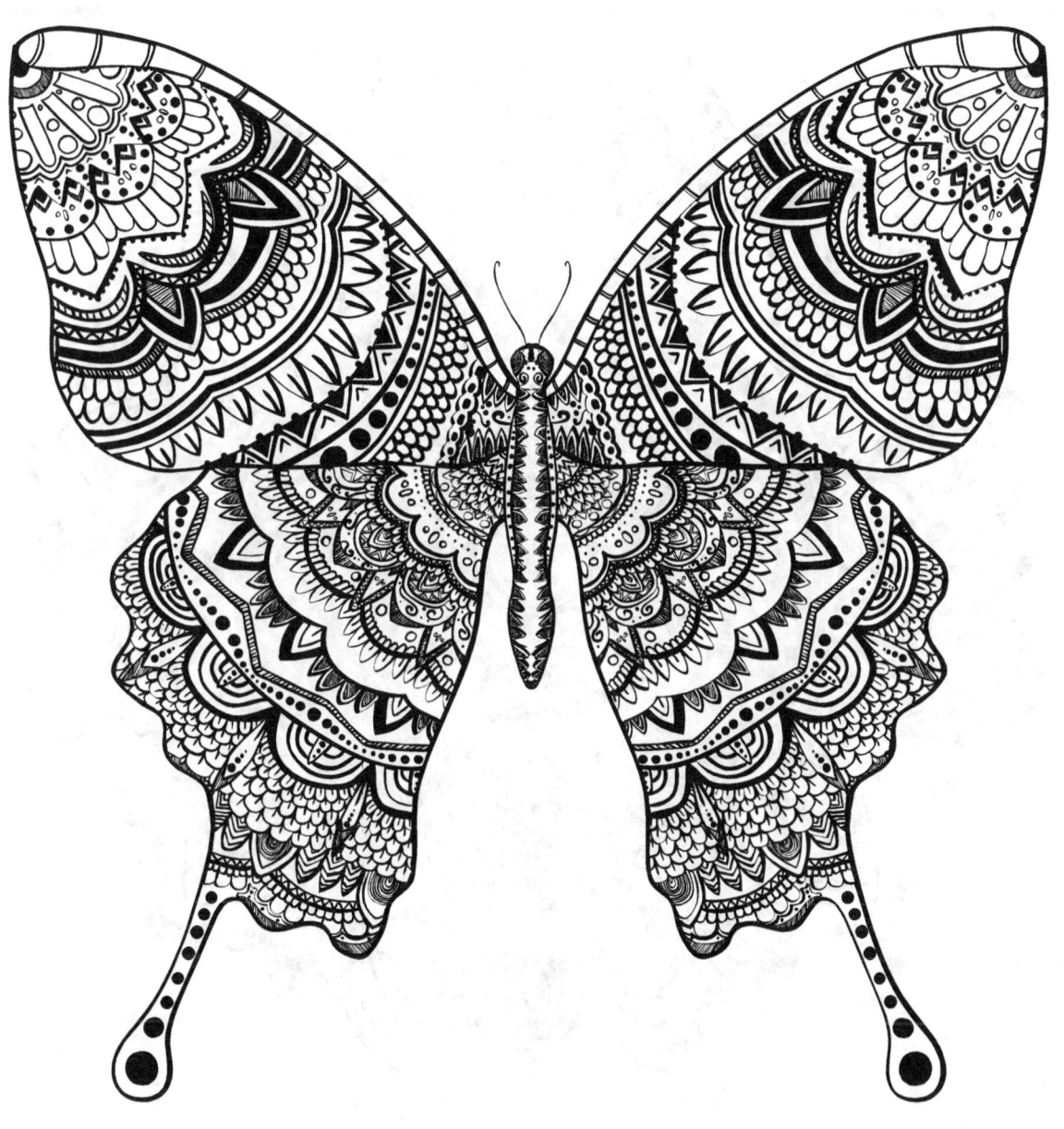

Orange represent vitality, excitement and change. Fill it in with a palette of tangerine, apricot, rust , ginger and amber.

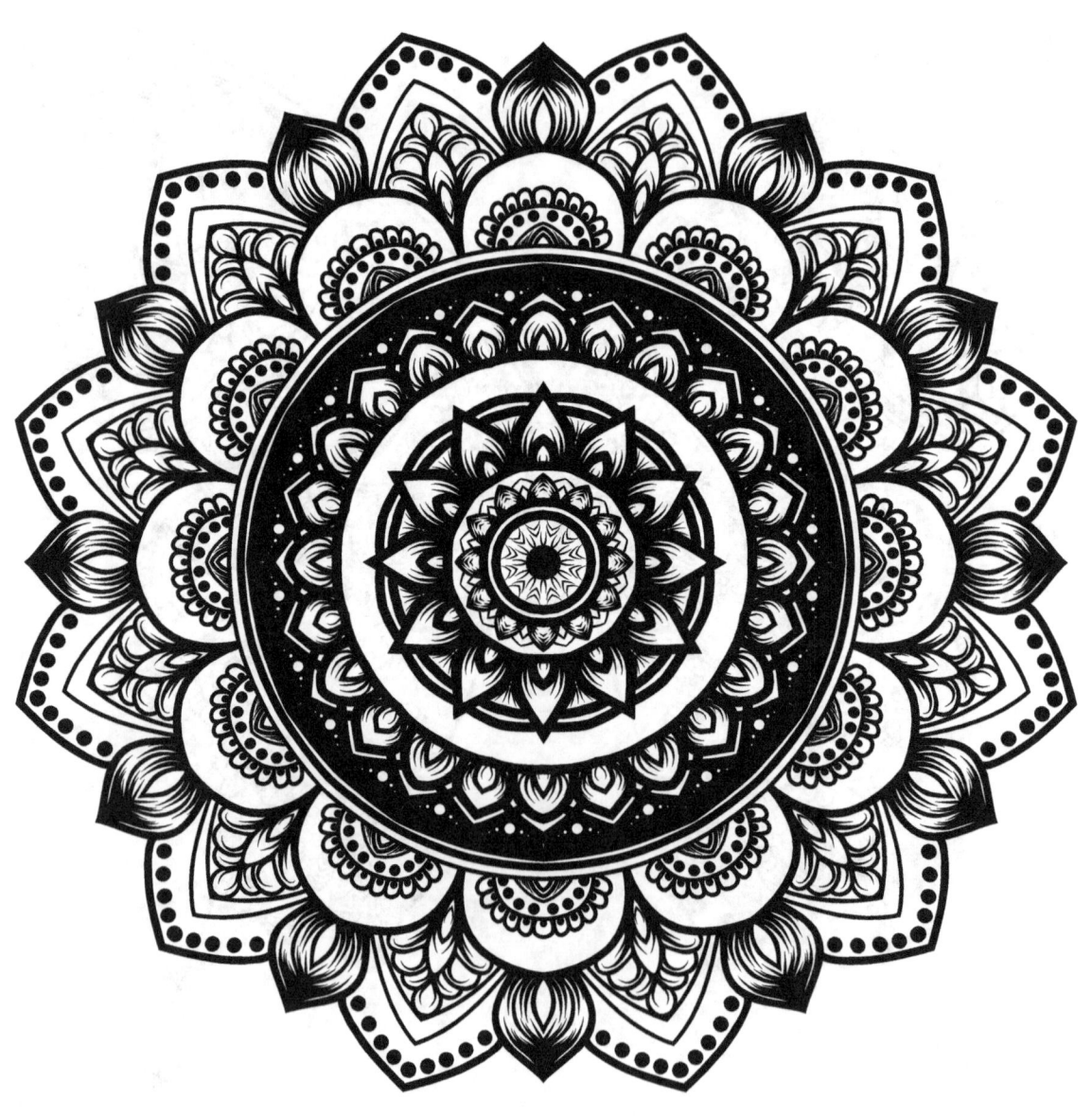

Fill in with a beautiful sunset scheme. Add a couple
purples, blues, orange and yellows.

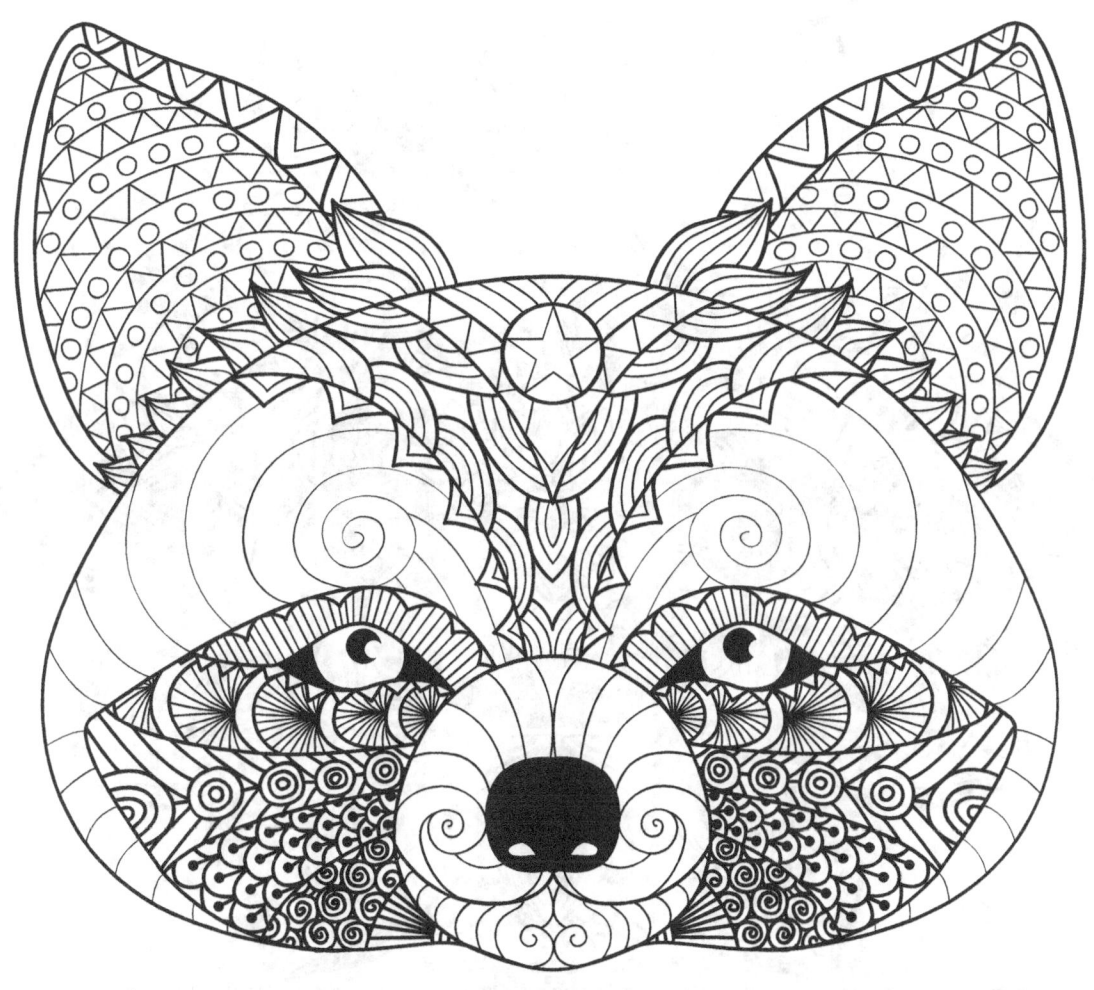

Fill in with a colorful pattern of waves.

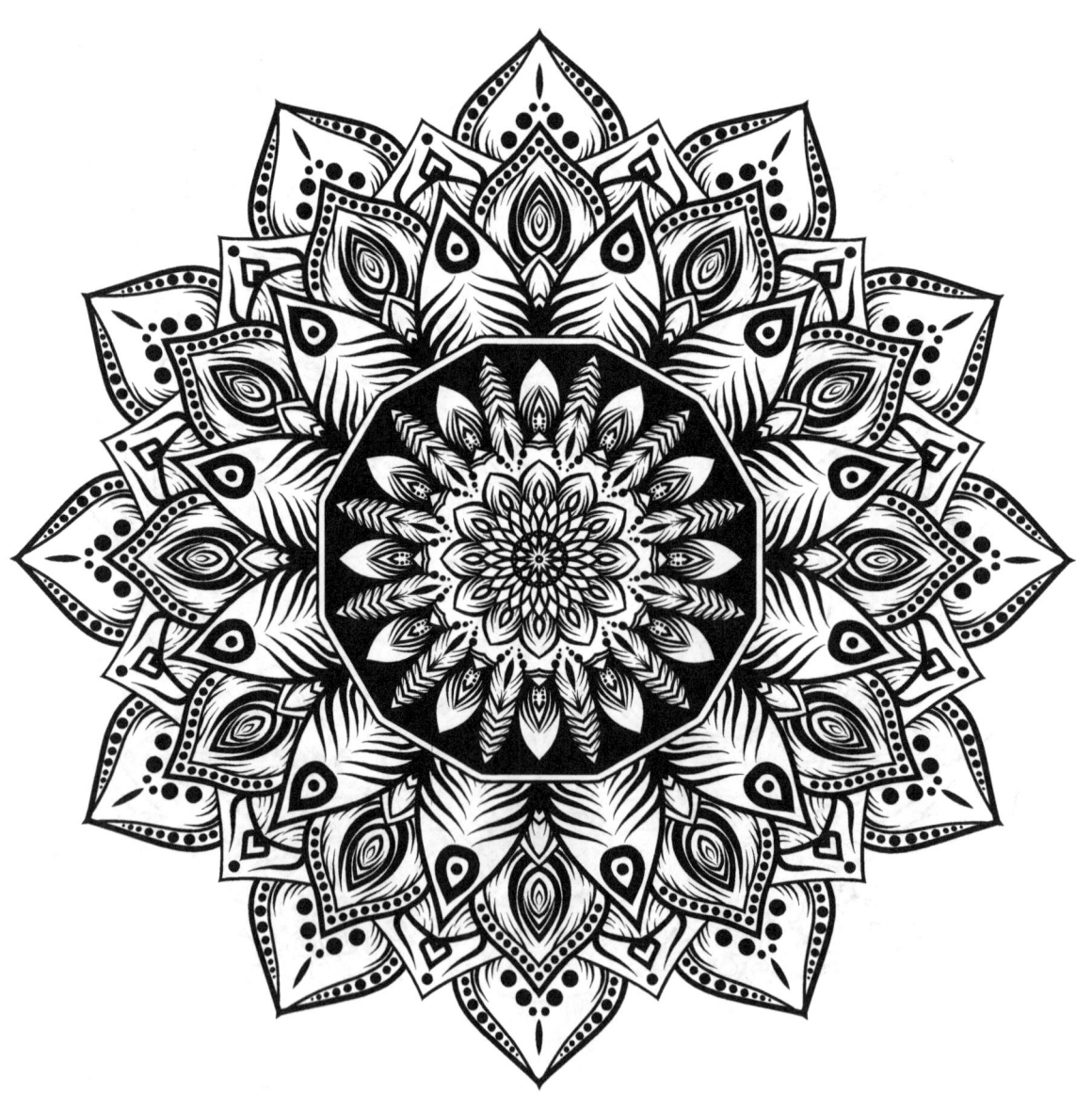

This will be living coral underwater palette. Add sea foam green, pink orange, light sea green and sea blue.

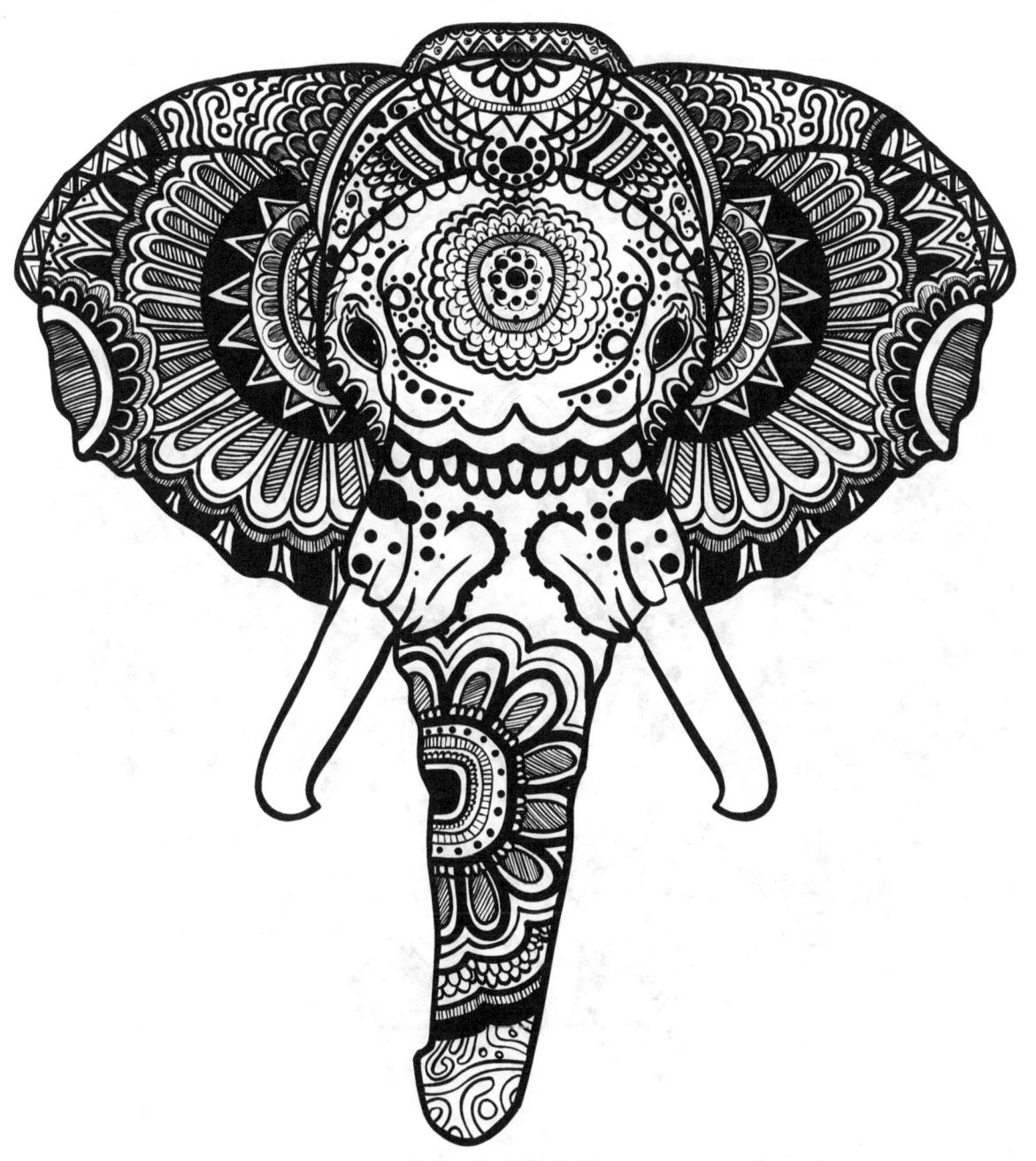

Paint the palette of your favorite cartoon character.

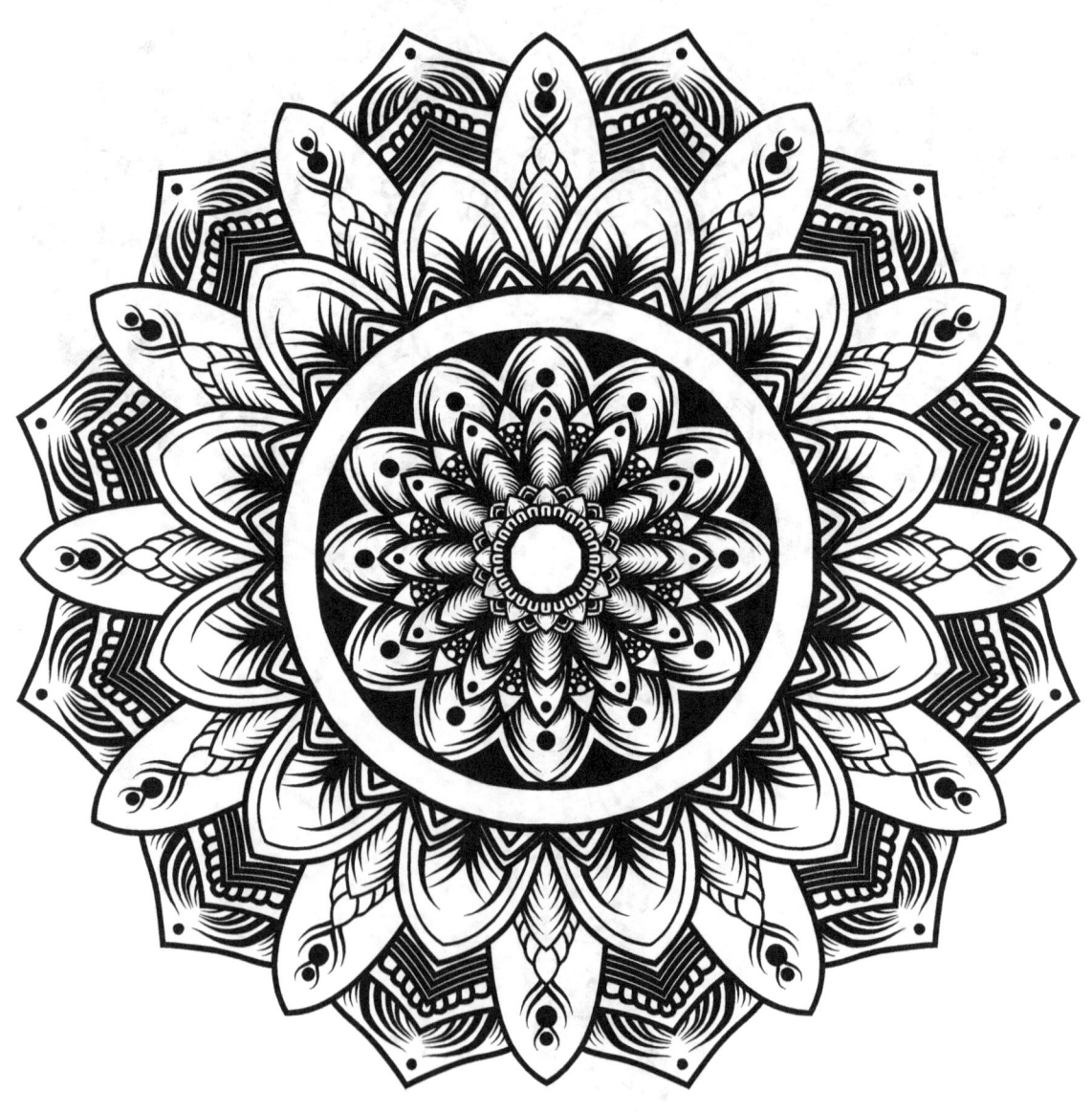

Nutty brown palettes from almonds to walnuts, chestnuts and cashews.

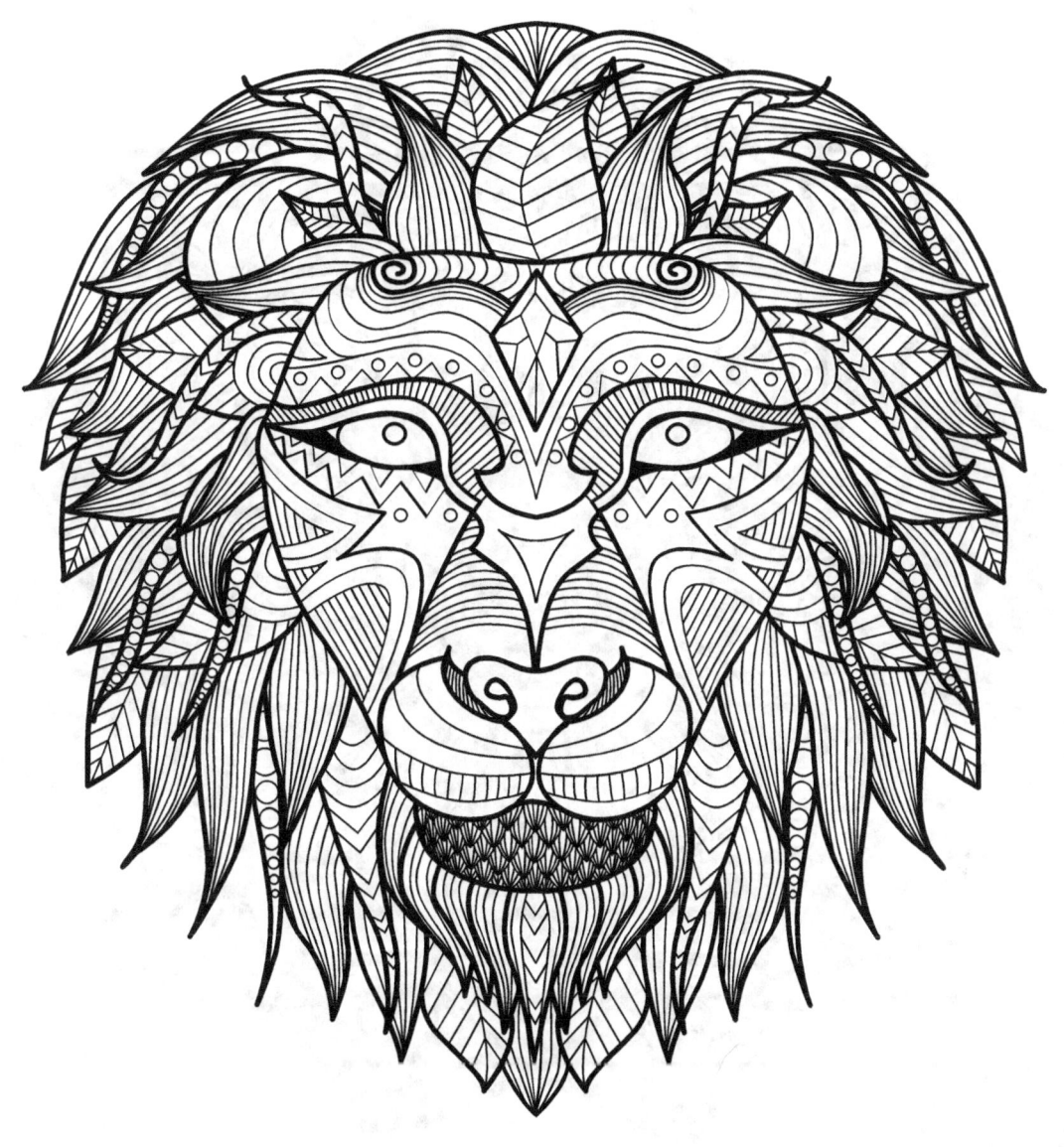

Go with warm tones including Cafe au lait, Cafe boil, cadmium orange and Cambridge blue.

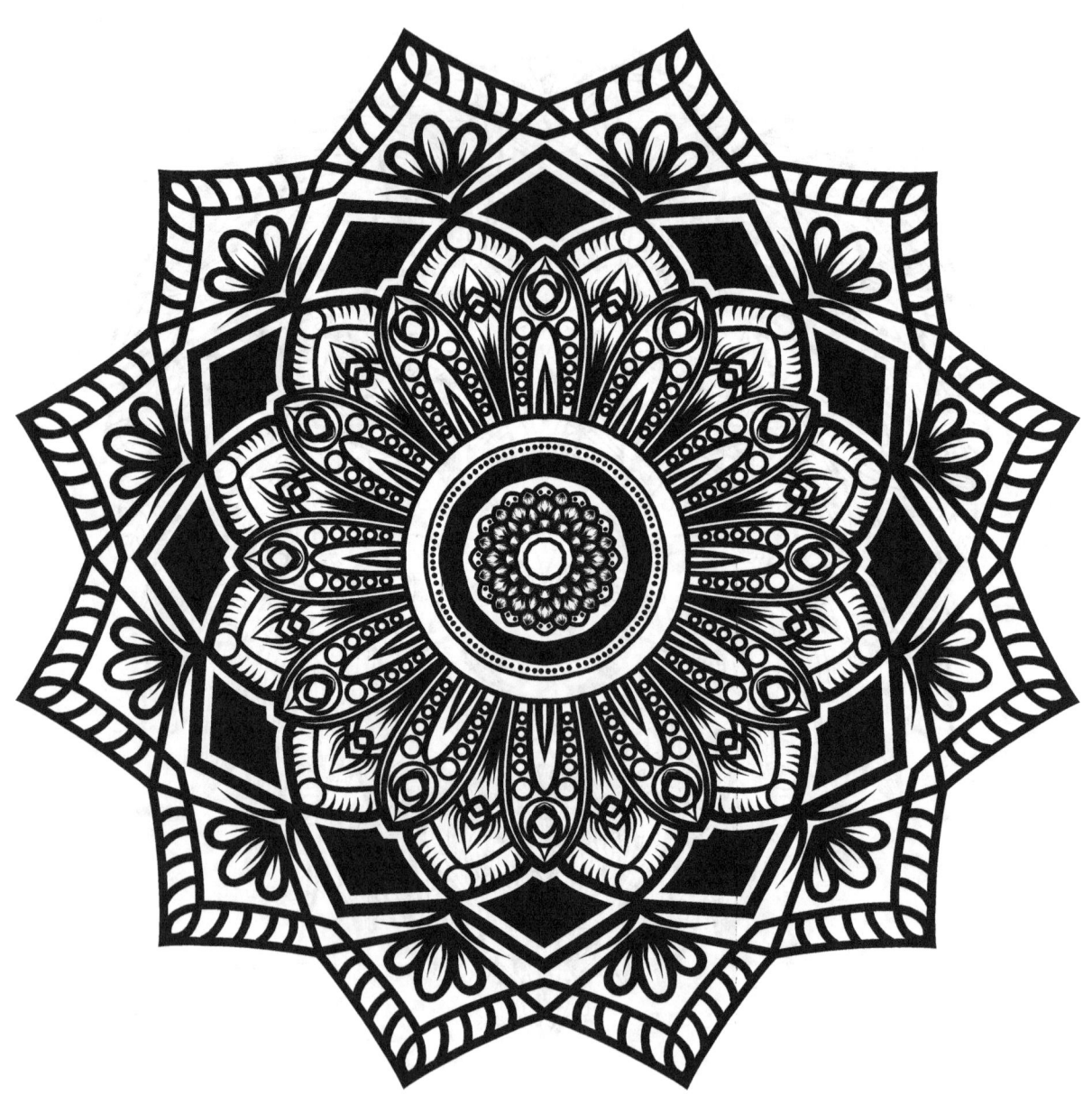

Color as fresh as garden. Think of Flowerbeds and vegetable plots. Make a yellow tinted green palette. Celery, lemon, kiwis are supporting cast members.

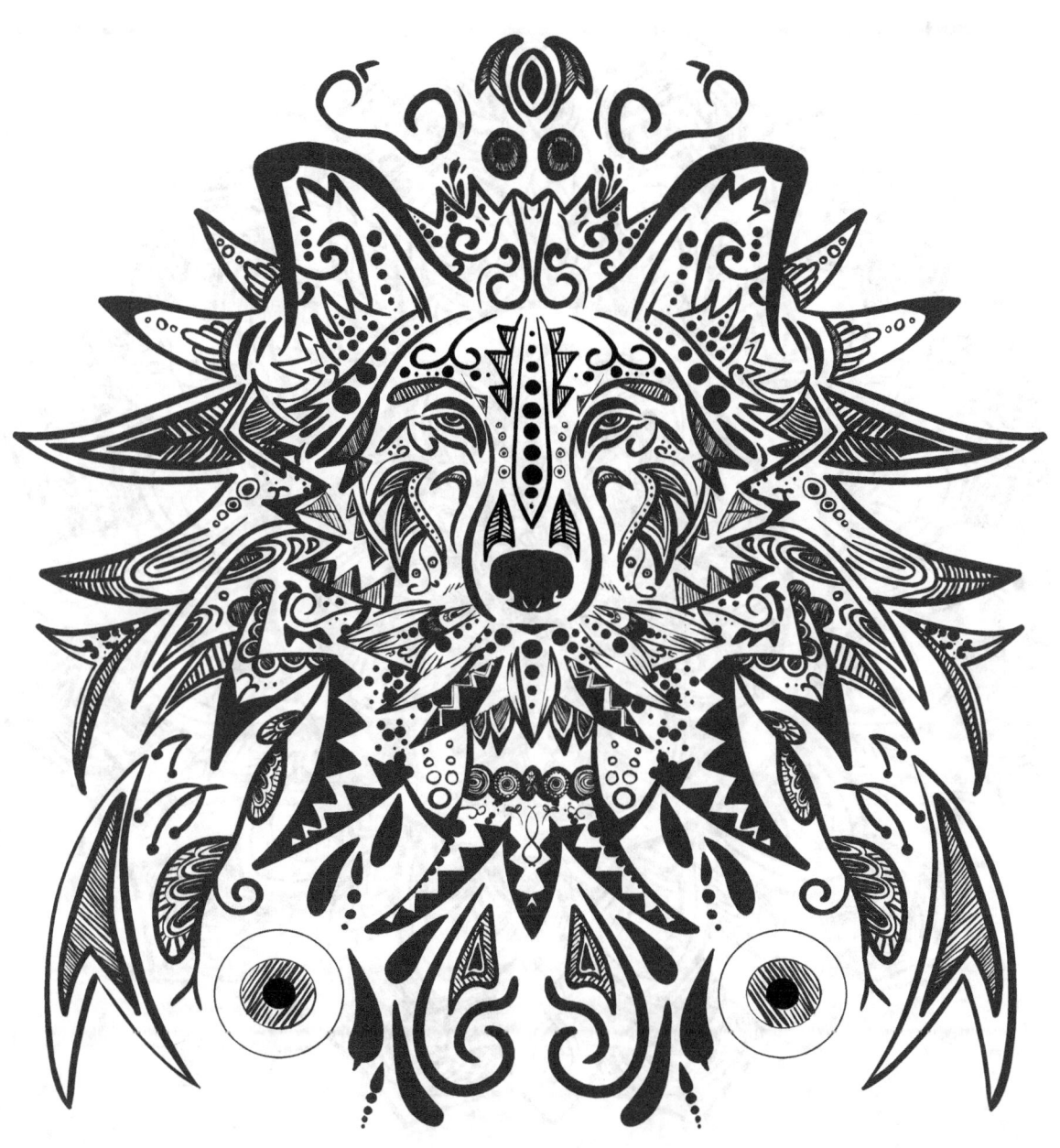

Paint the colors of the best gift you have ever got.

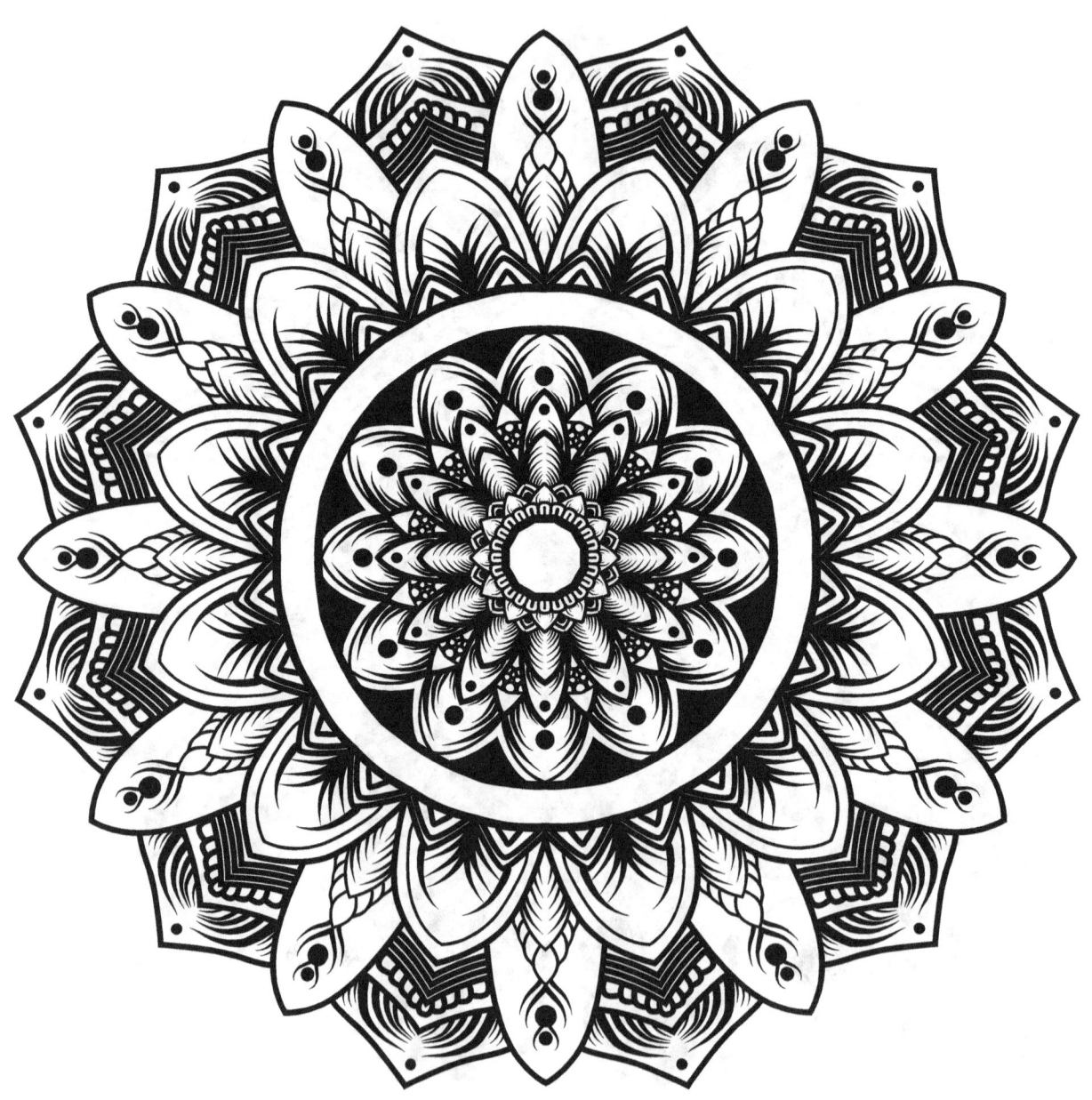

The calming hues of the ocean waves; varying between green and blue based on light and weather. Include the soothing blues, turquoise, aqua teal, baby blue and azure.

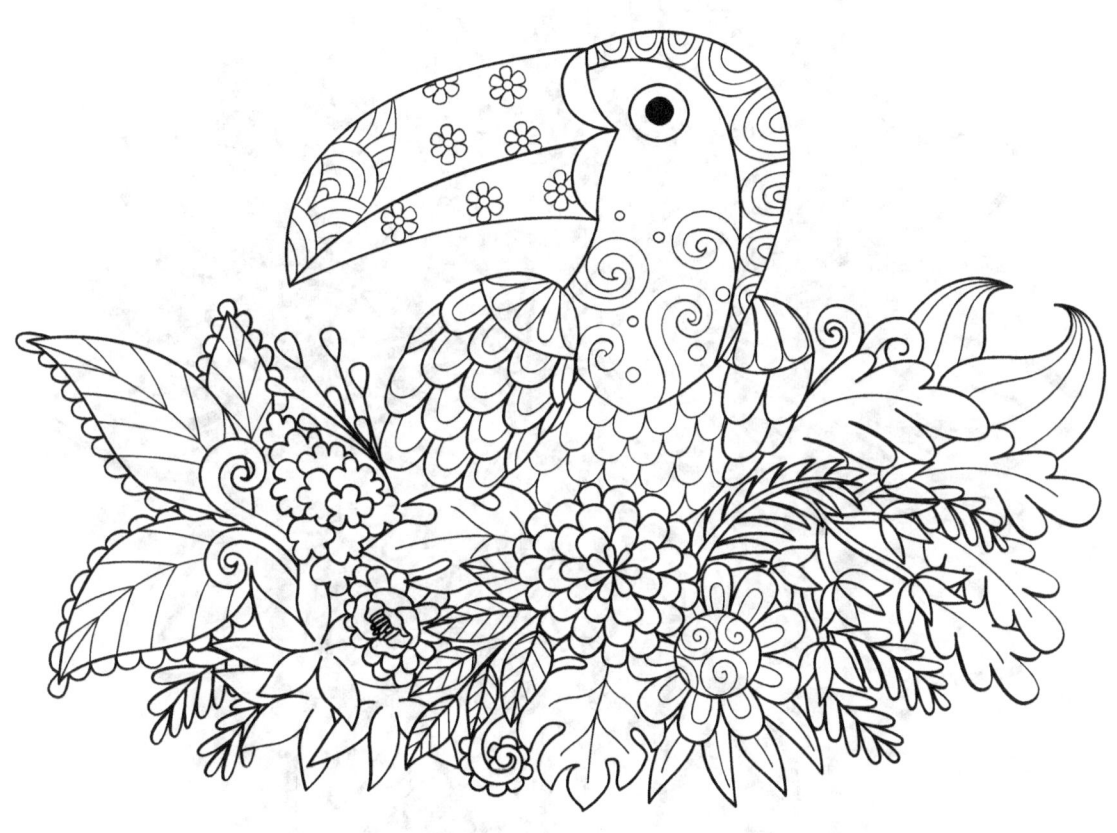

Add colors that you want to see in a makeup palette.

Think of peacock beautiful plumage. Add beautiful hues of vibrant green, blues and purple. Top it off with gold, magenta and copper.

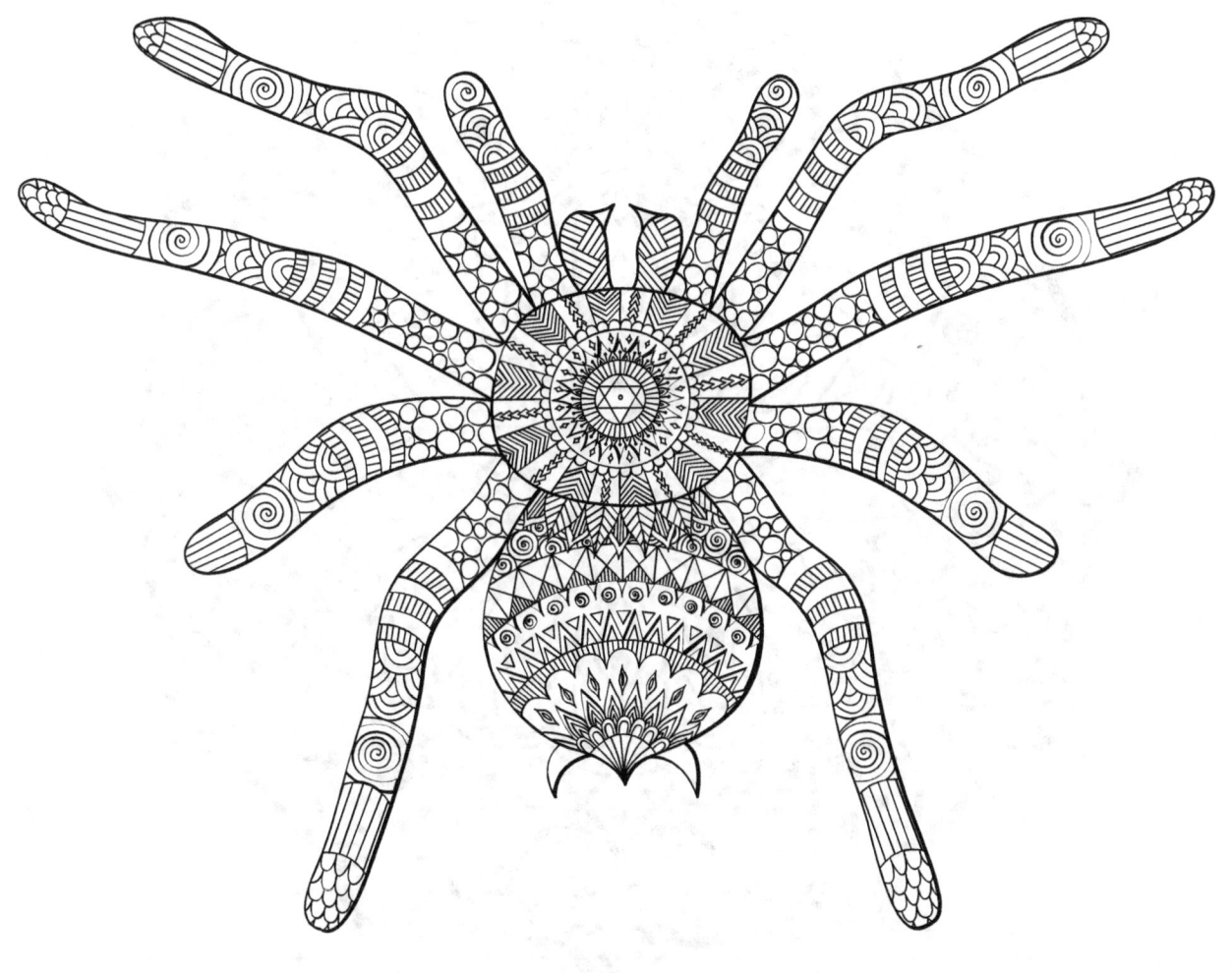

Funk this page up with artic green, Aureolin, aqua and aquamarine.

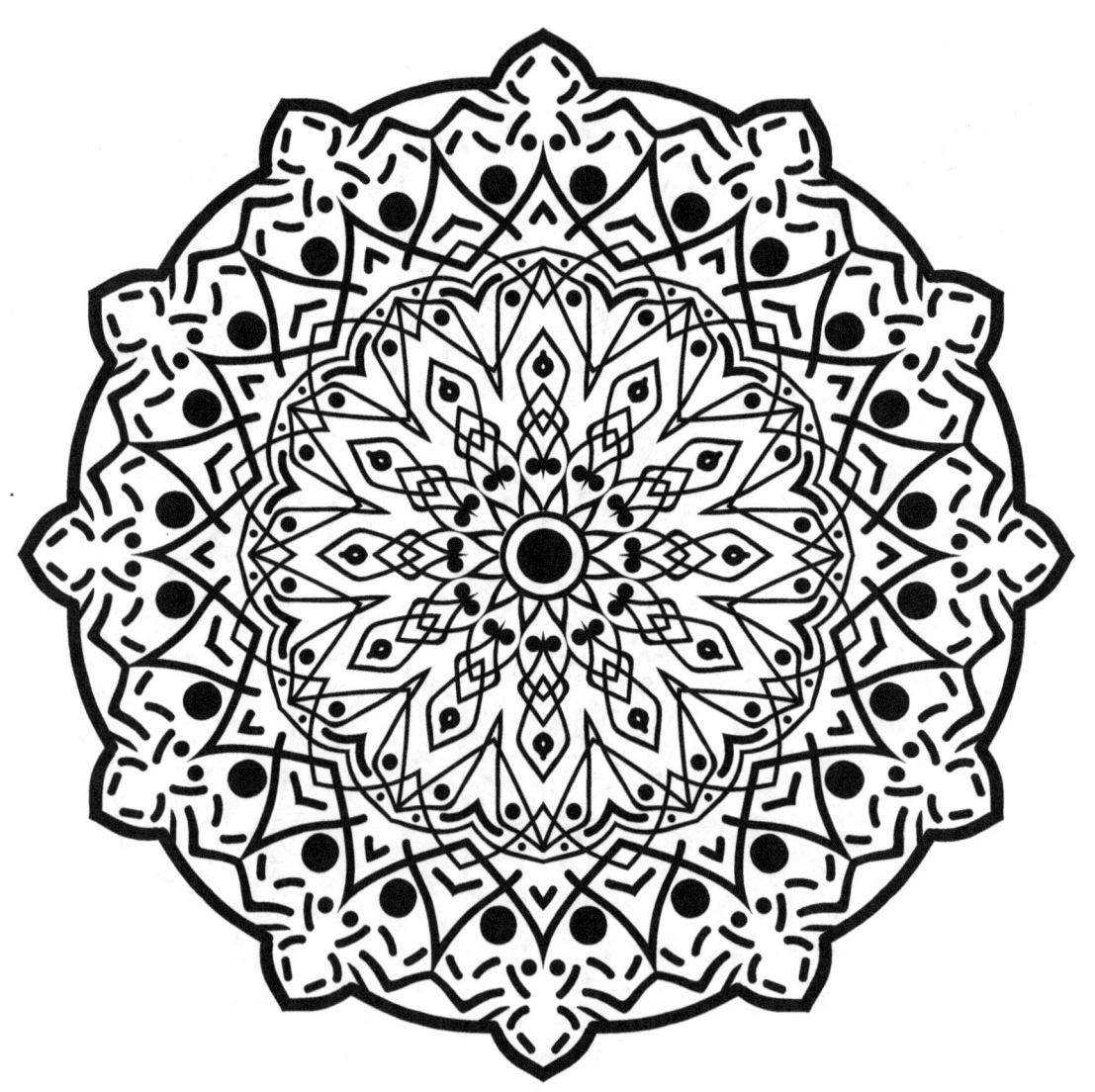

This of the land of fire and ice. Capture Iceland legendary beauty in this palette. Add warm grayish undertones with bright green contrast. Add a range of lighter and darker shades to make colors that compliment each other.

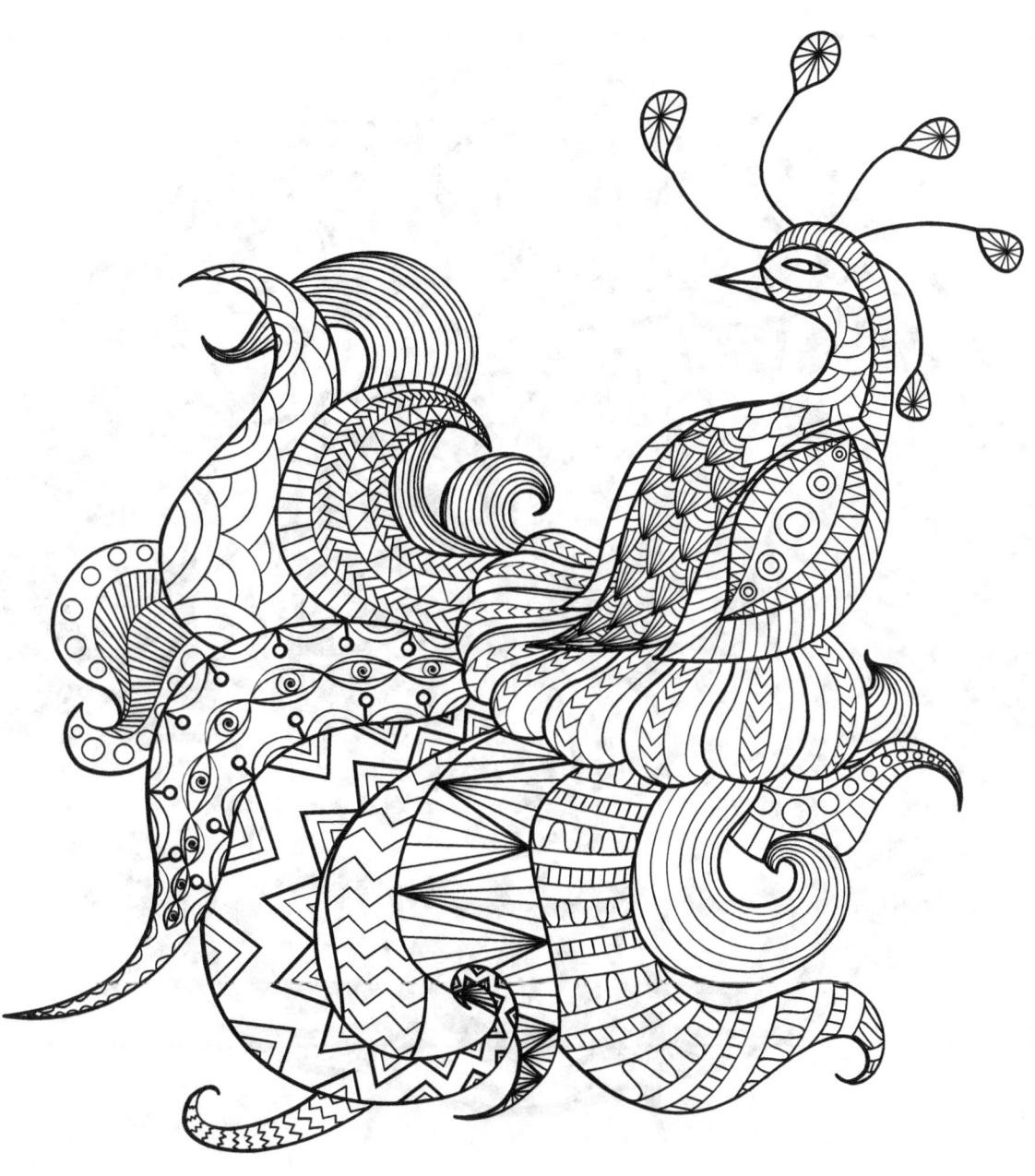

Color will a palette of your choice with parallel strokes.

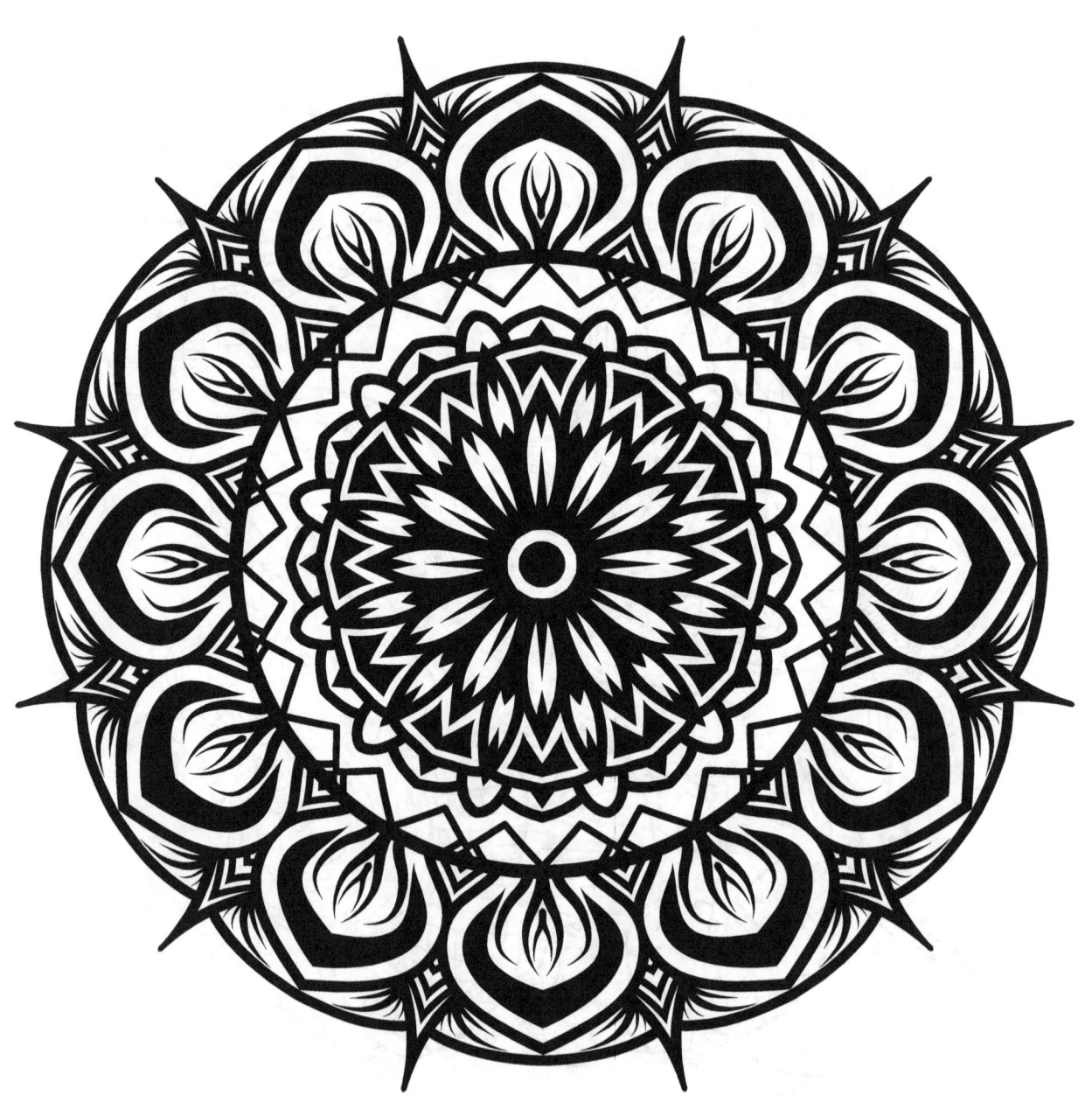

Add earth and lime and grass and forest green. Think
of it outdoorsy and natural.

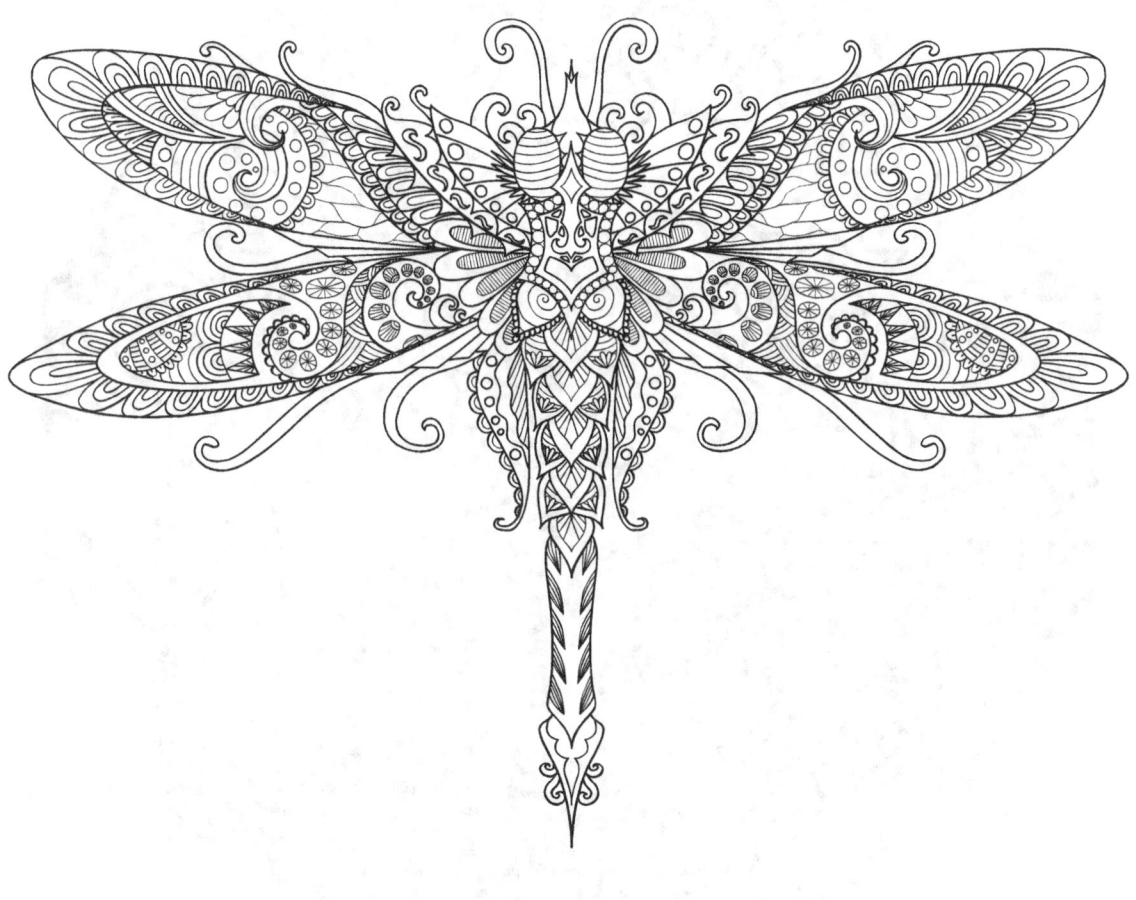

Use the cluster of hatched limes to fill this in.

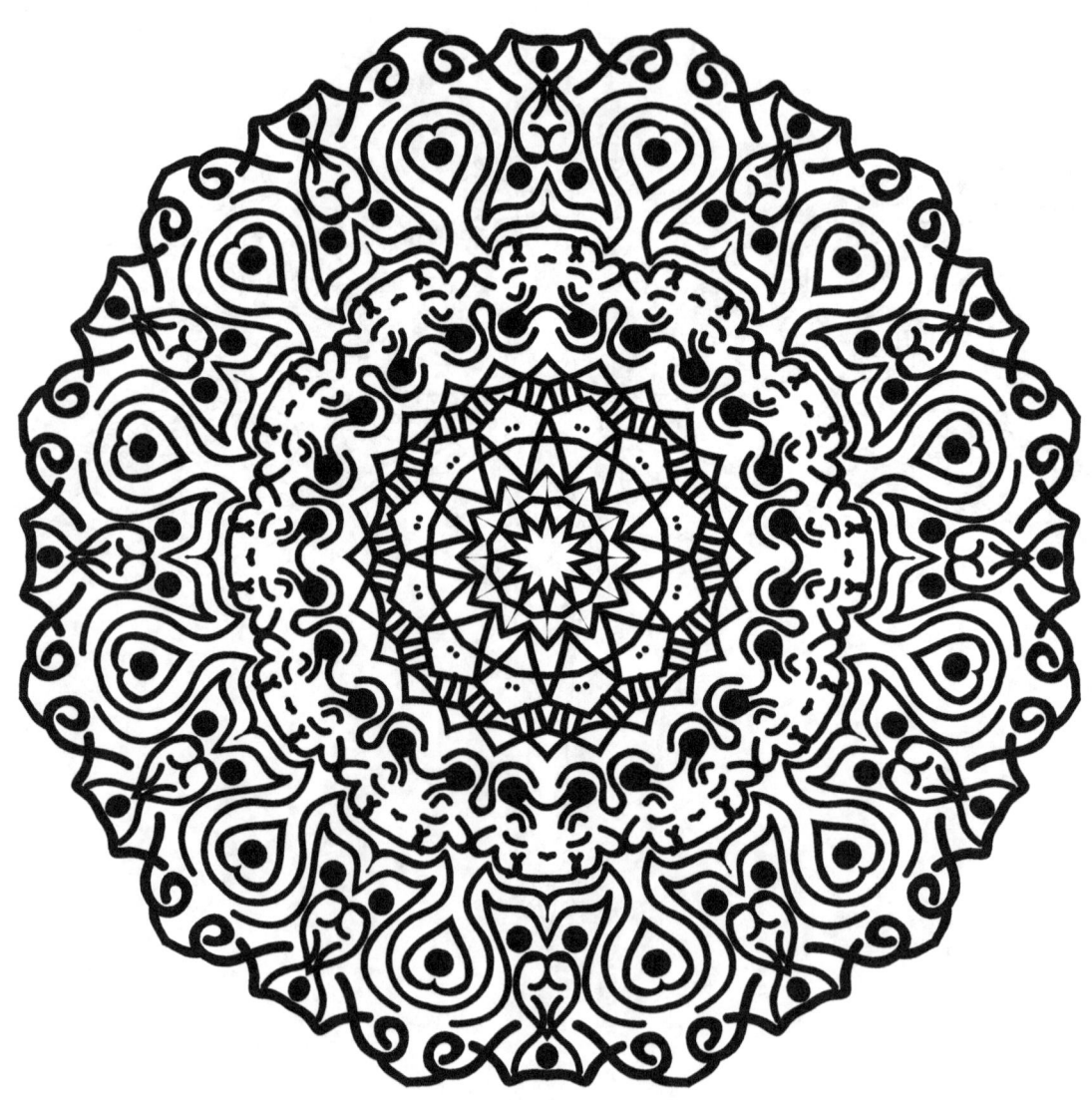

Think of Grand Canyon. Add dramatic orange brown contrasts of desert landscapes. Pair it with plums and red clay orange.

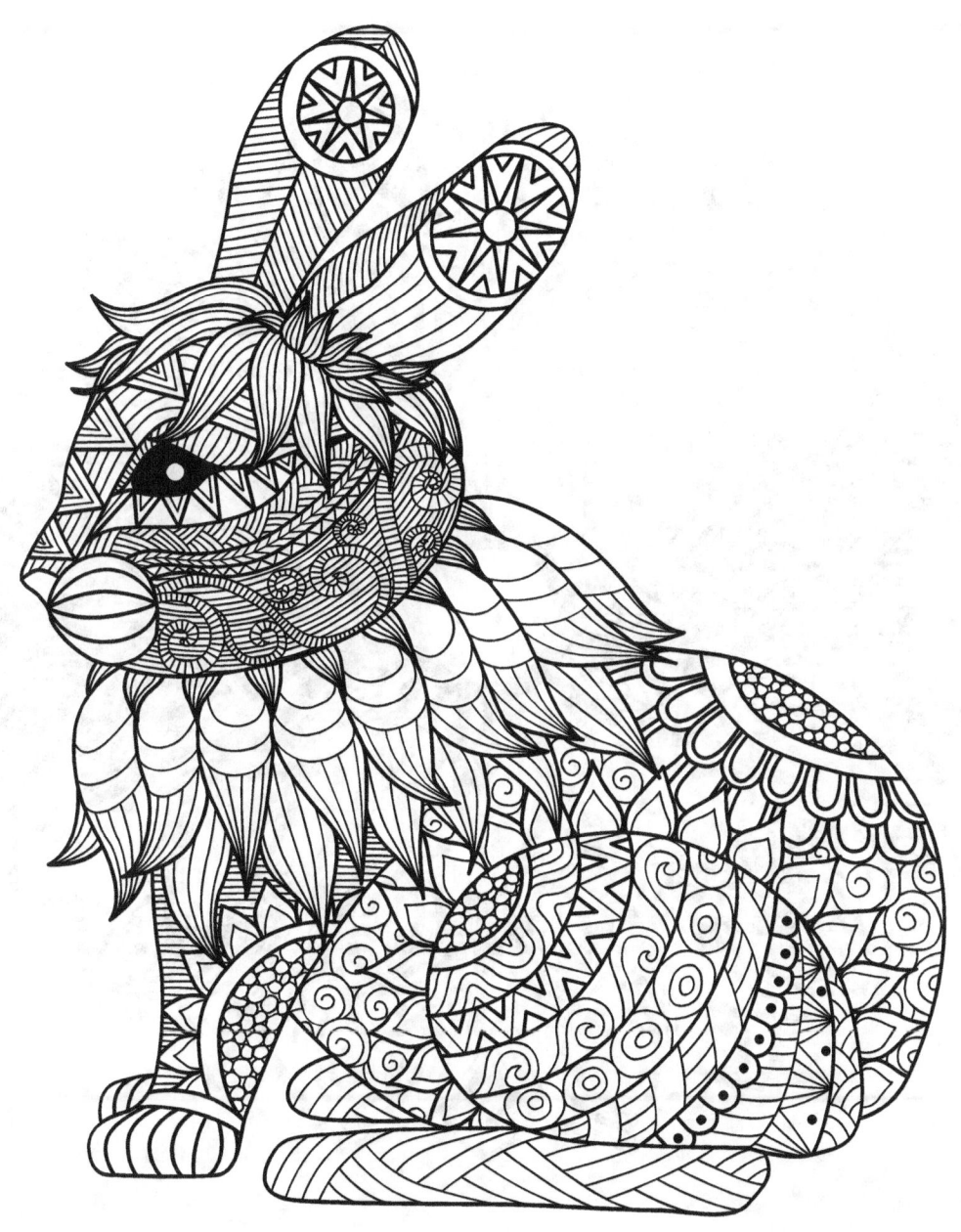

Pick colors from the Grand Canyon.

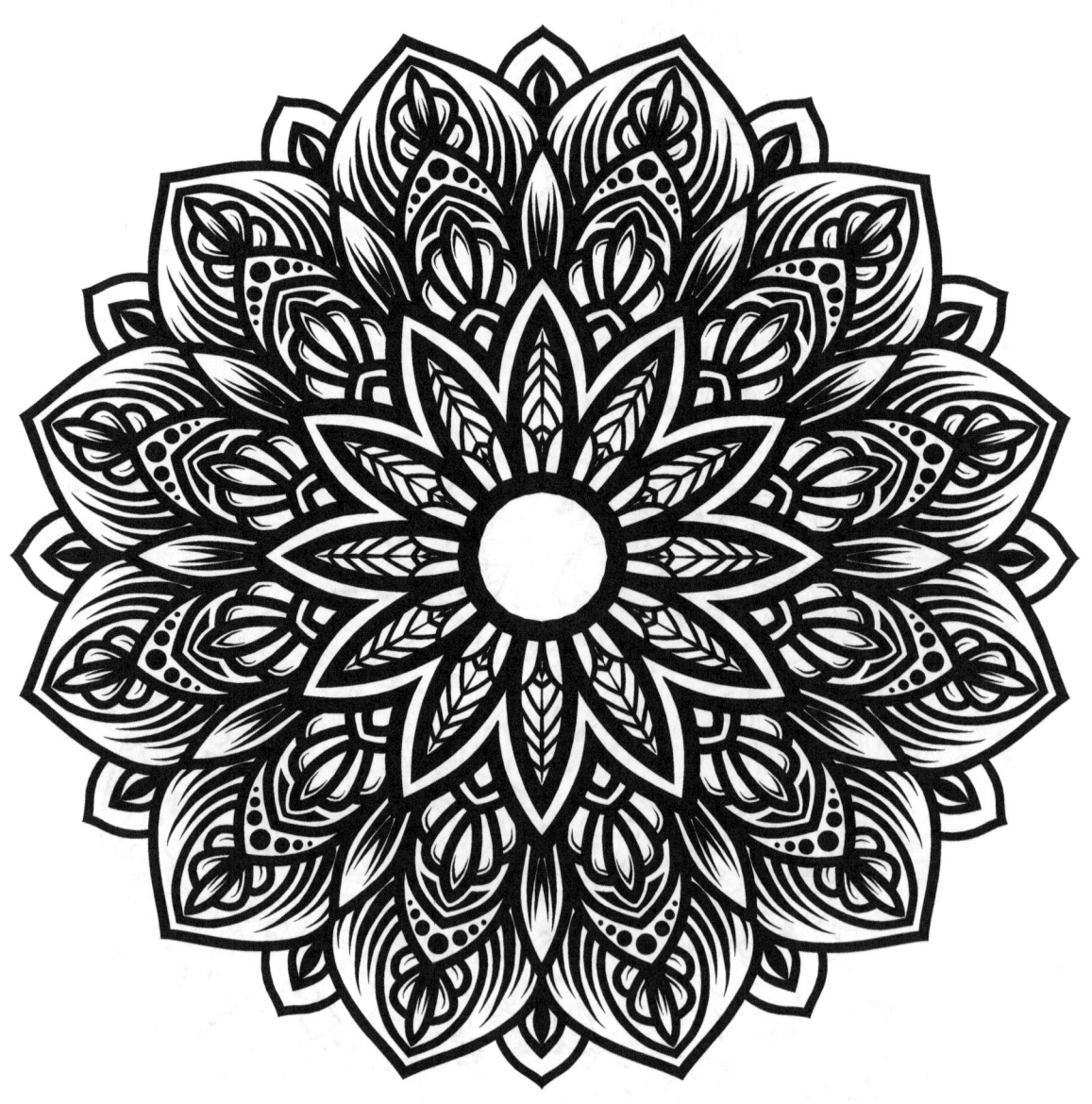

Go basic, go primary. Basic colors have eye catching power. Add various shades of reds, blue, green and yellow.

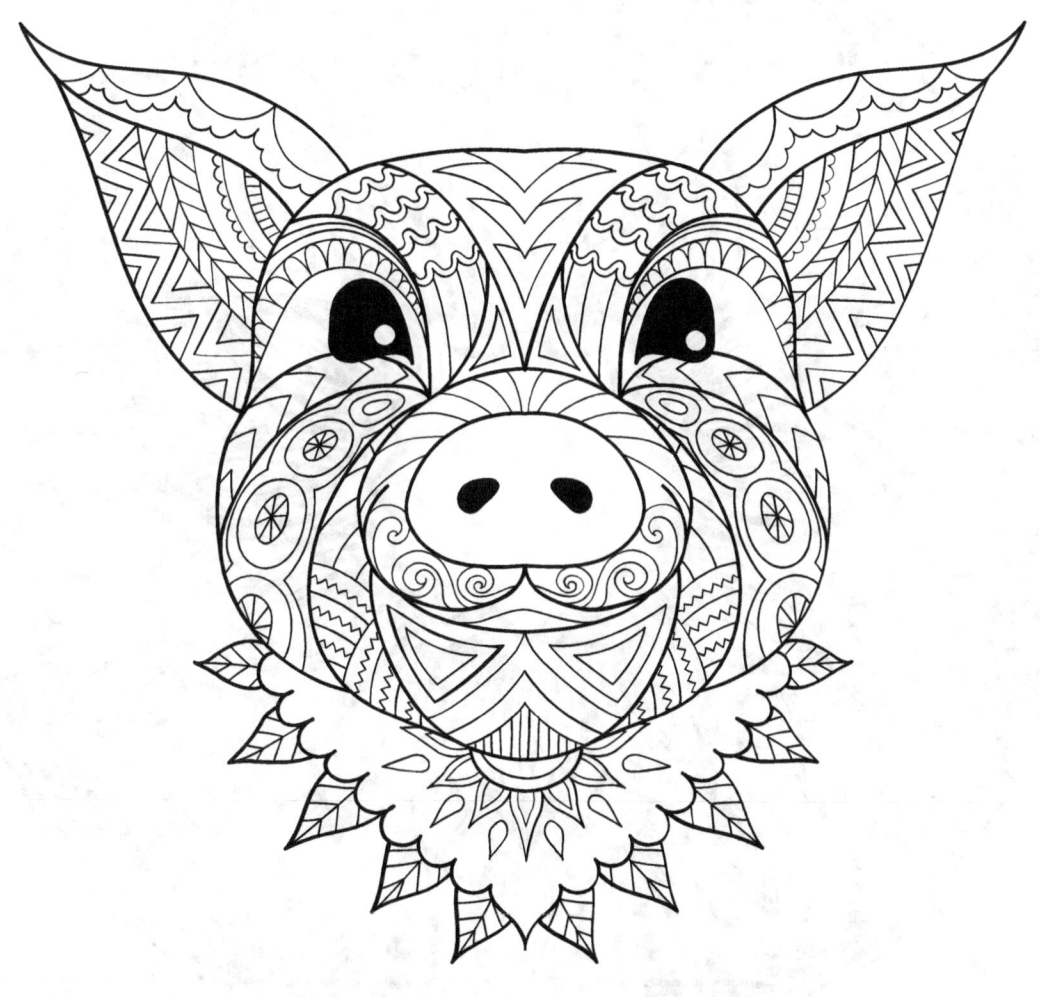

Picture yourself standing on a beach at sunset.
The sky is ablaze with colors of oranges, pinks,
and purples.

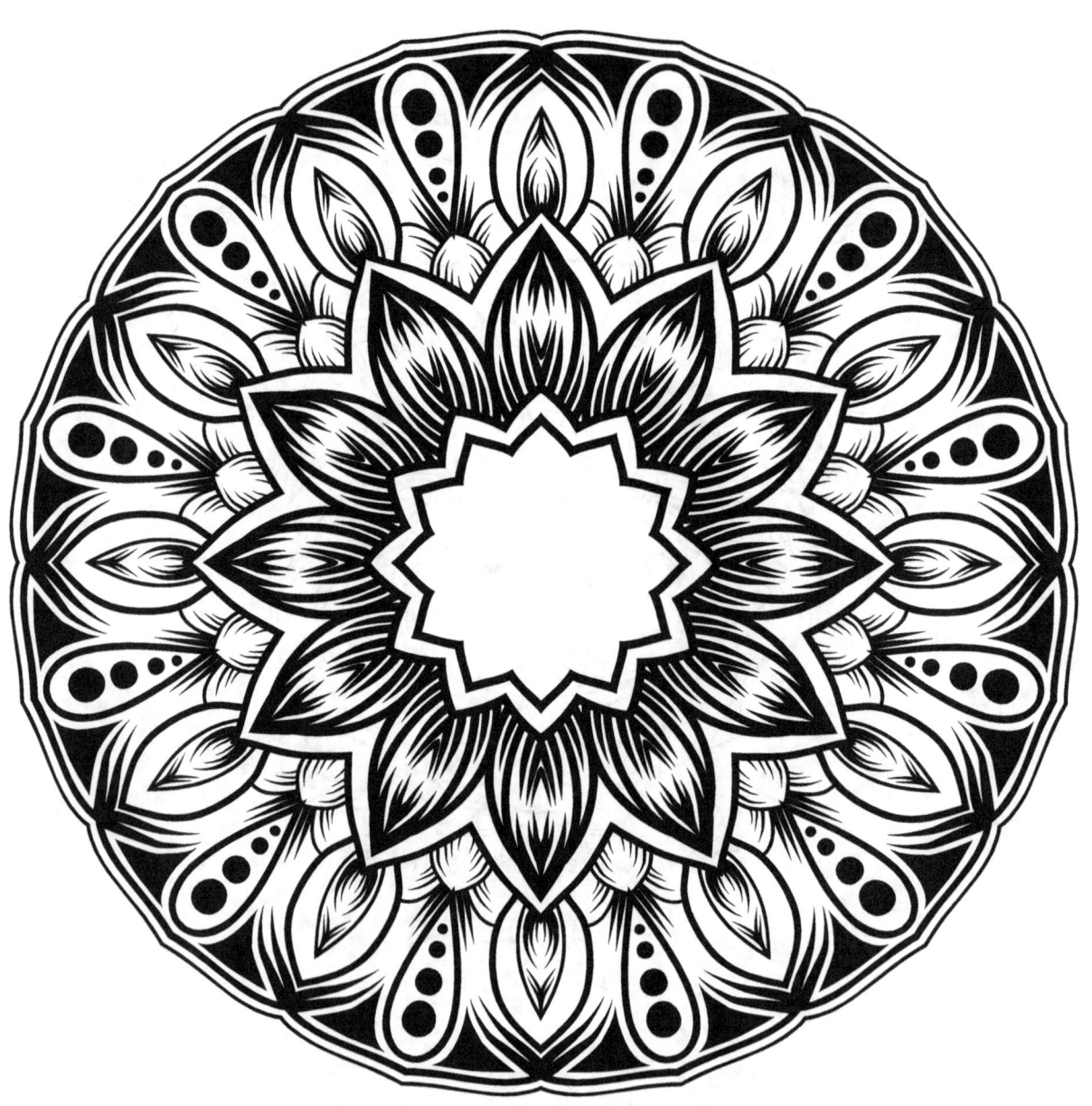

Bright yellow and bubblegum pink contrast sharp turquoise colors for a palette that is almost Easter candy-like. Pair it up with aquamarine hues for a fresh, clean look.

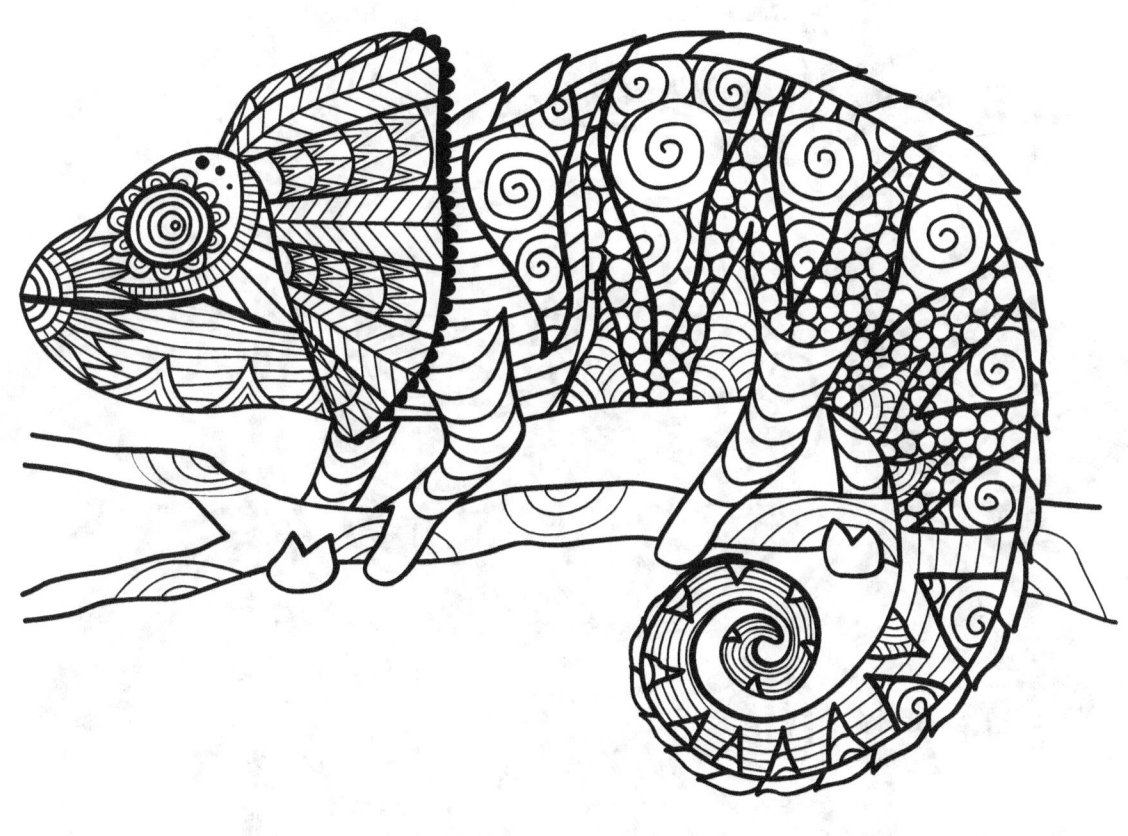

Apply pointillism. Fill in with the color of your choice by stippling.

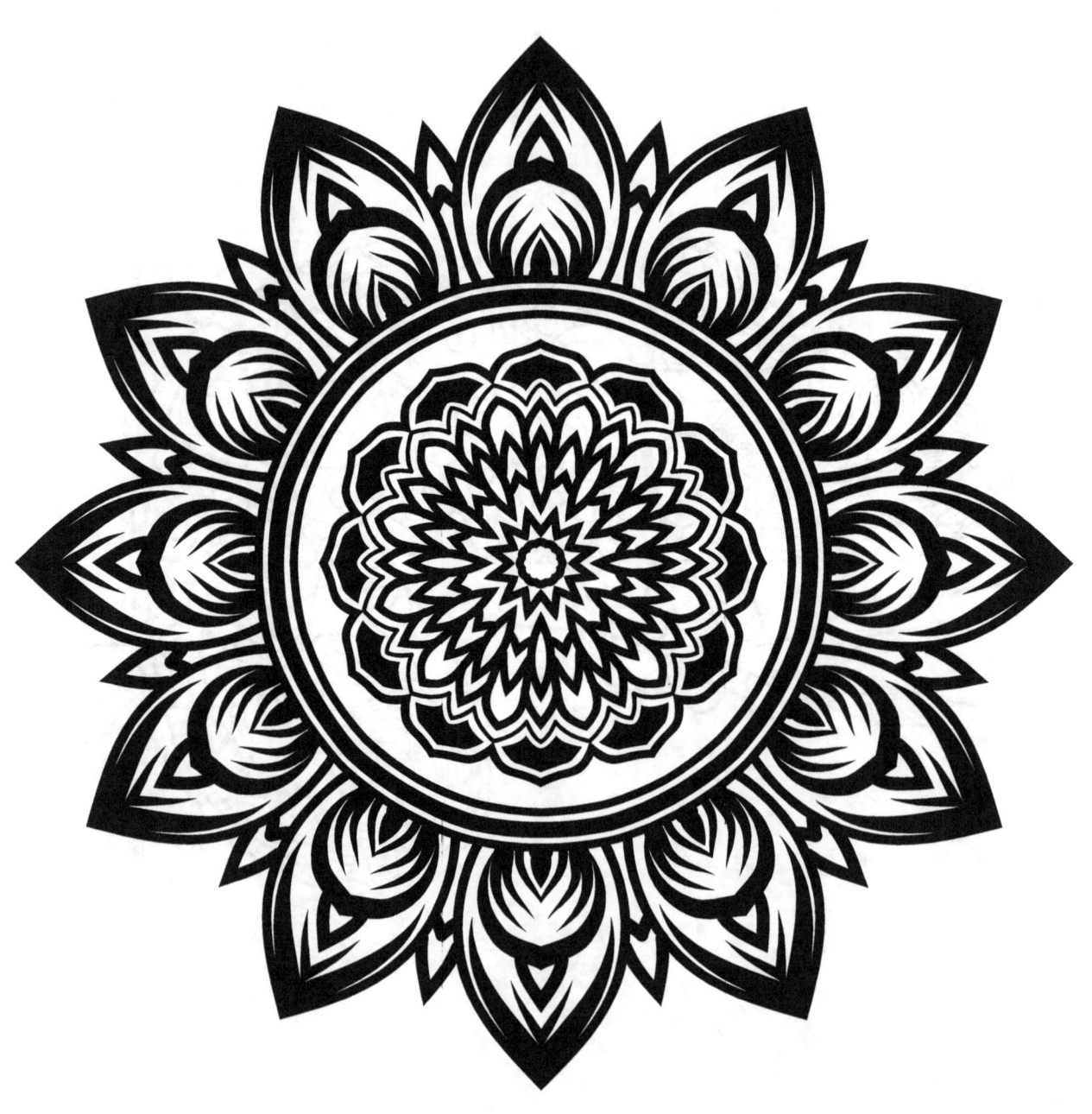

Its autumn in Vermont. Rust, gold, forest green and crimson hues evoke memories of the outdoors and have a rustic realness to them.

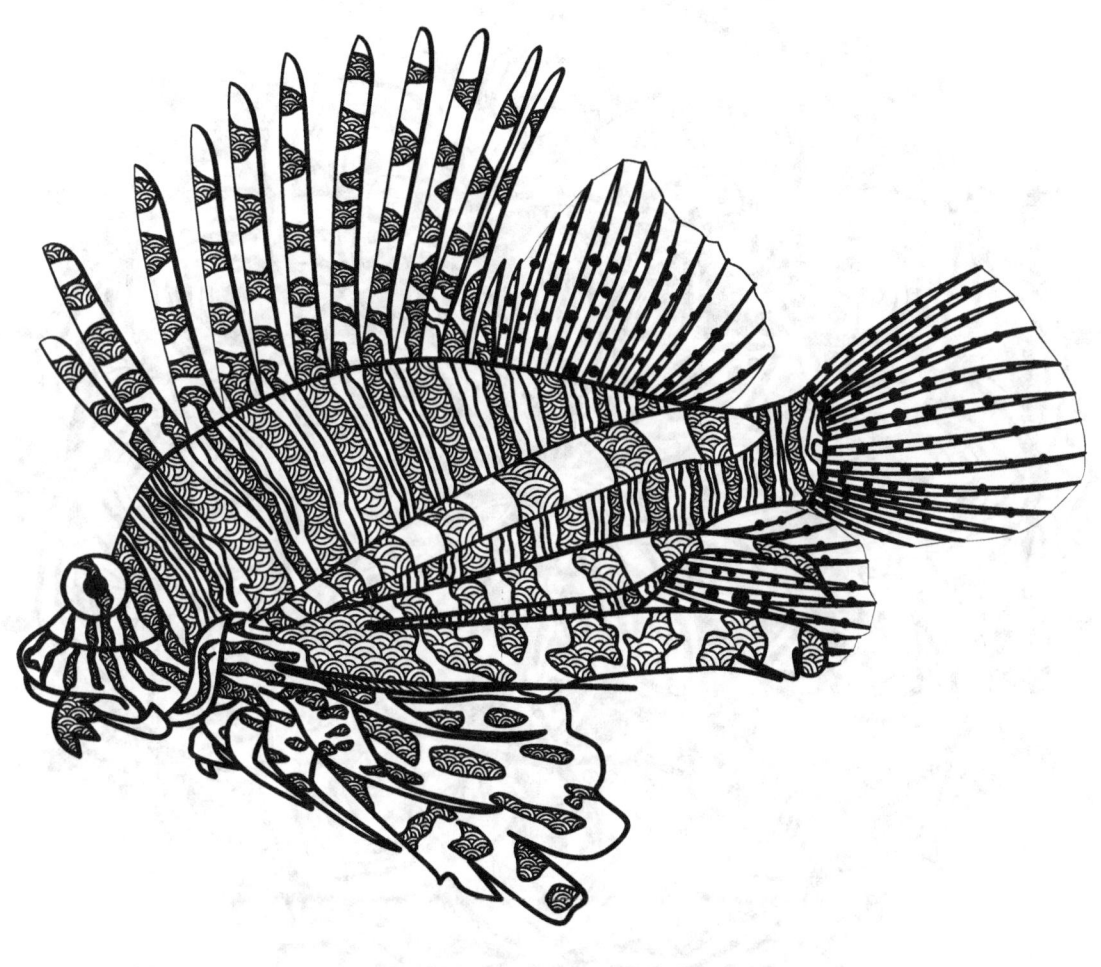

Cottagecore: Muted shades of green and brown for a warm, earthy feeling.

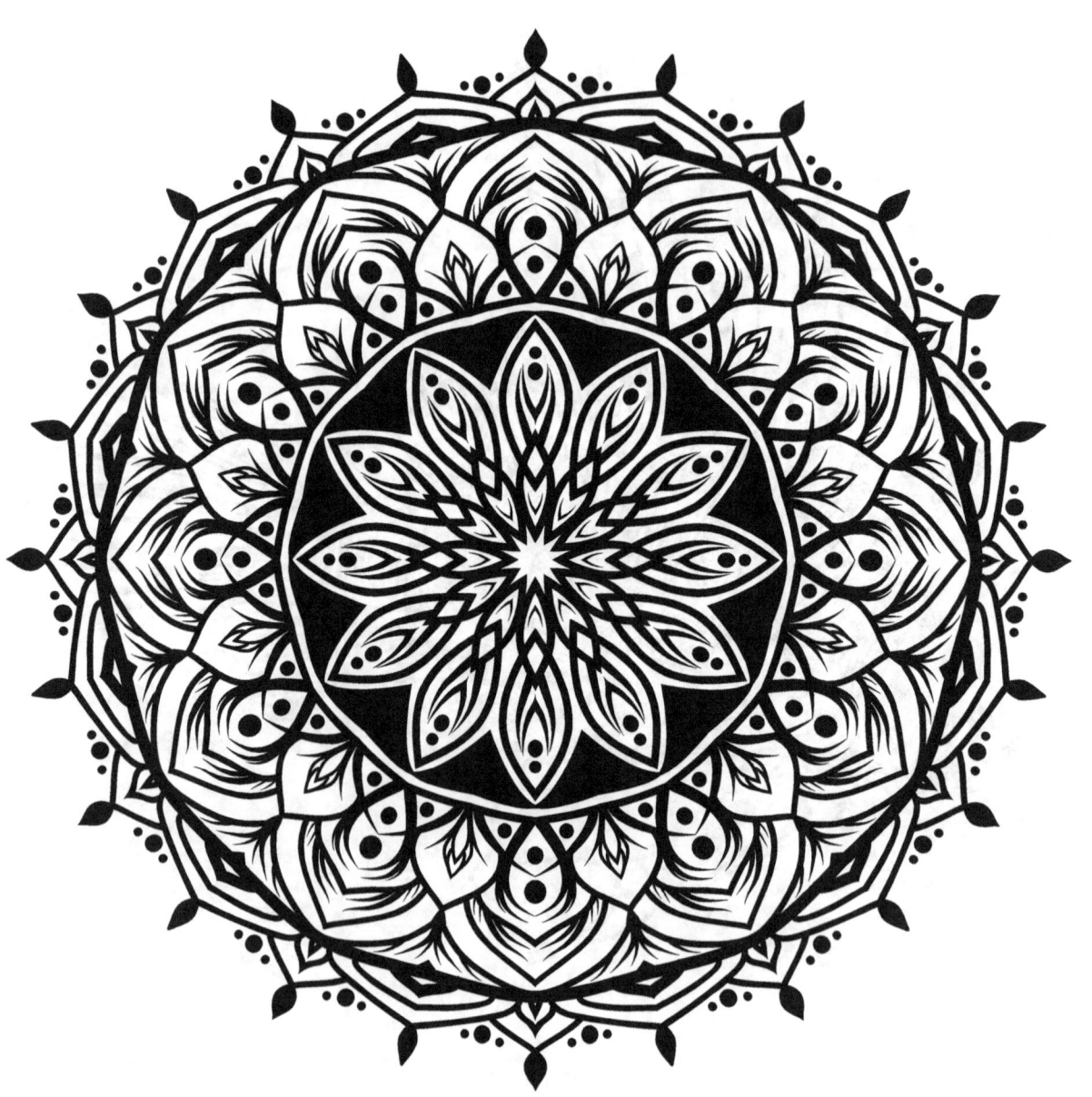

The icy glaciers. A dynamic color scheme is created by contrasting warm greys with icy, glacial blues. Try these lighter, brighter colors instead of navy and dark grey if you require a more restrained color scheme.

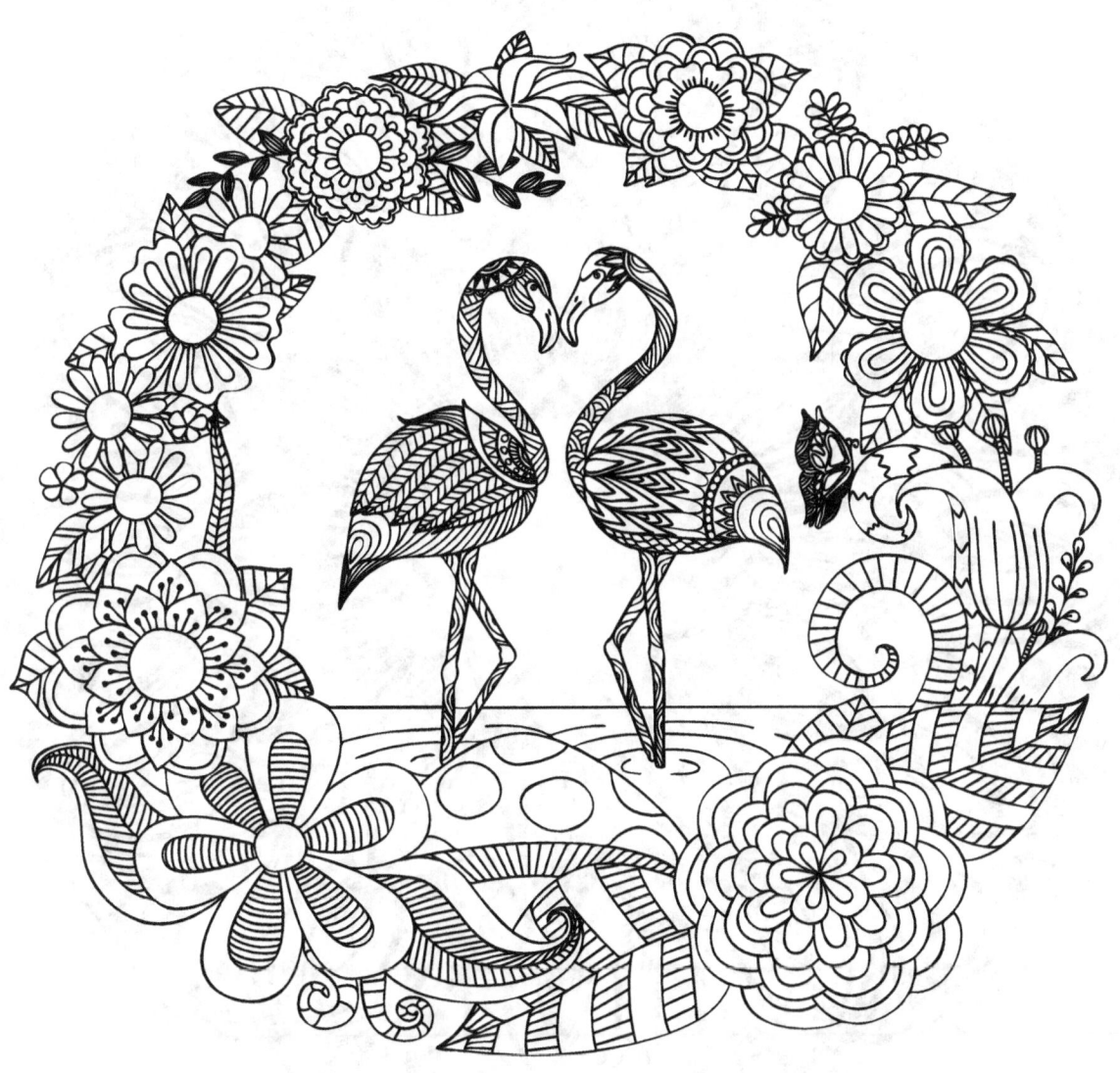

Scribble around with a rainbow of colors.

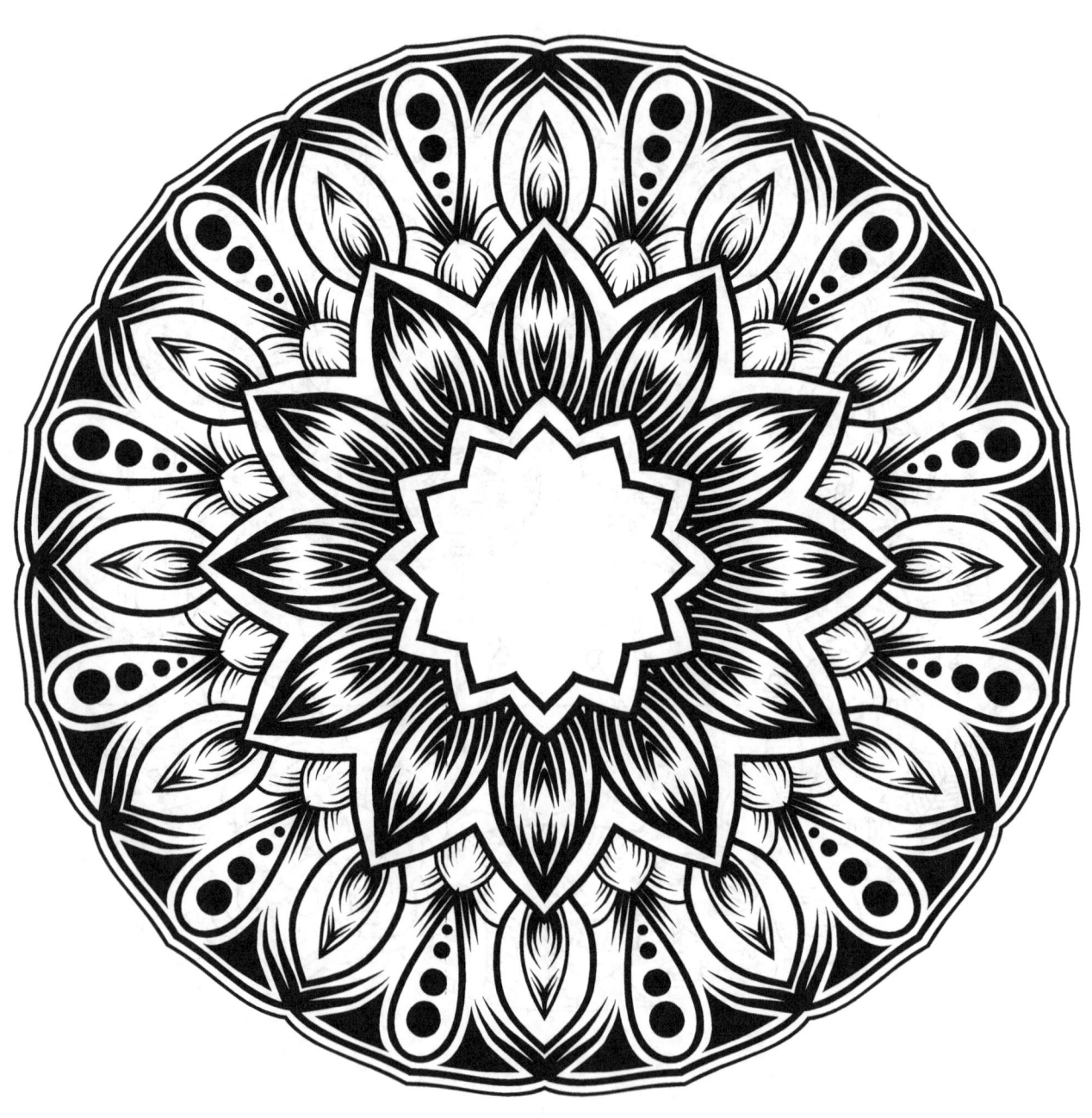

Go wild either your imagination on this page. Use any color.

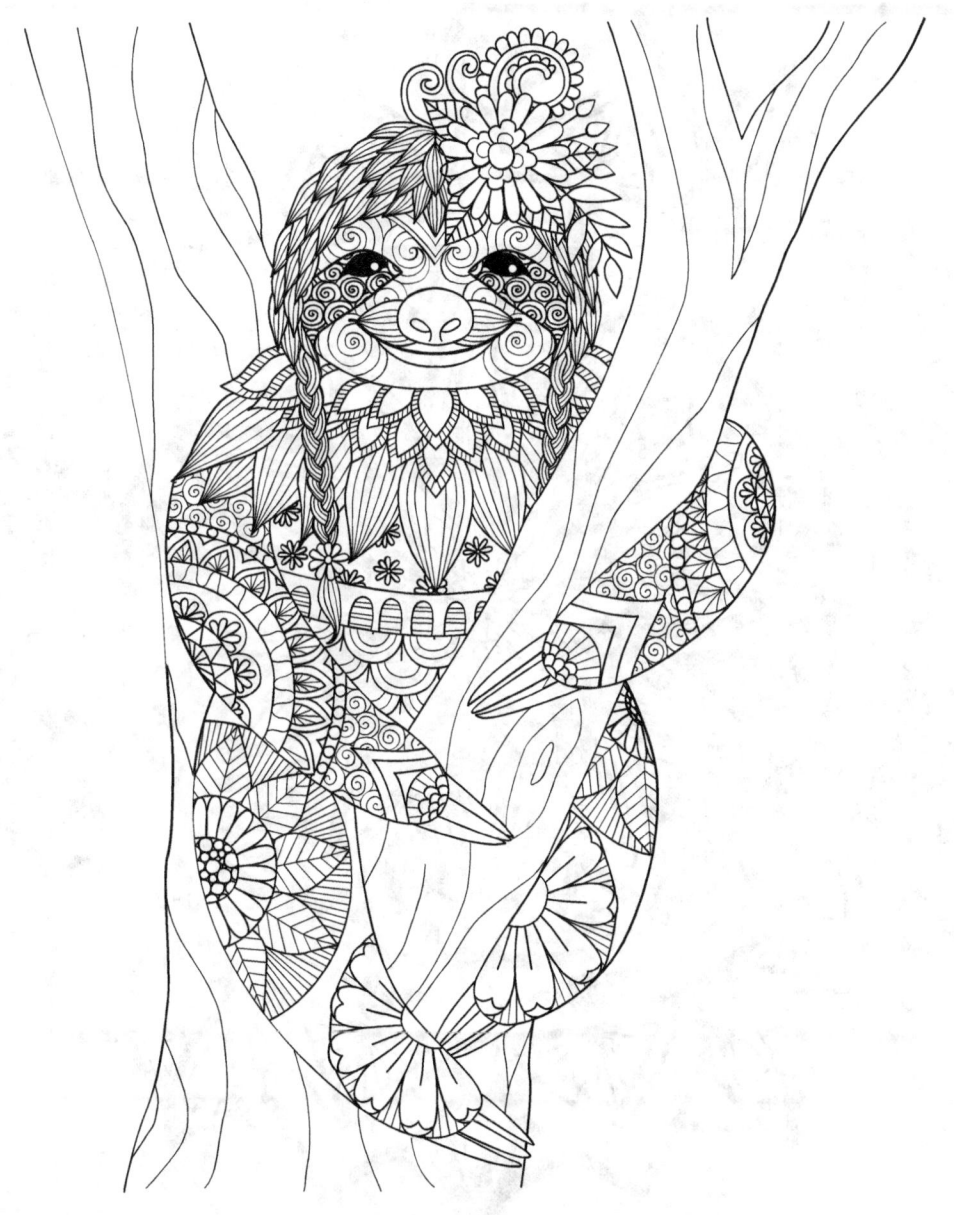

Envision a clear night sky full of twinkling stars.

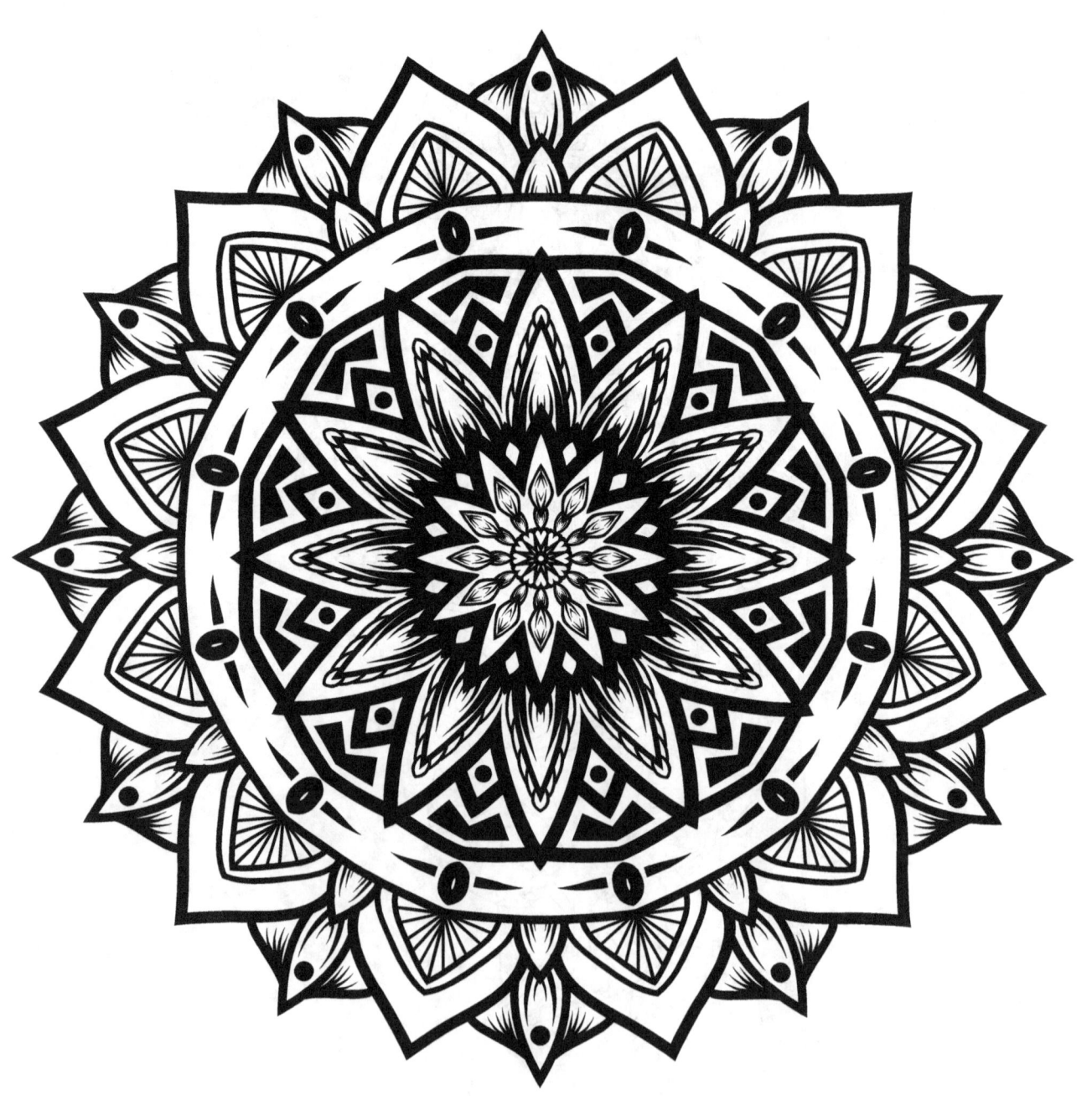

Keep it monochrome. But don't limit to Black and white.
Add various shades of grey.

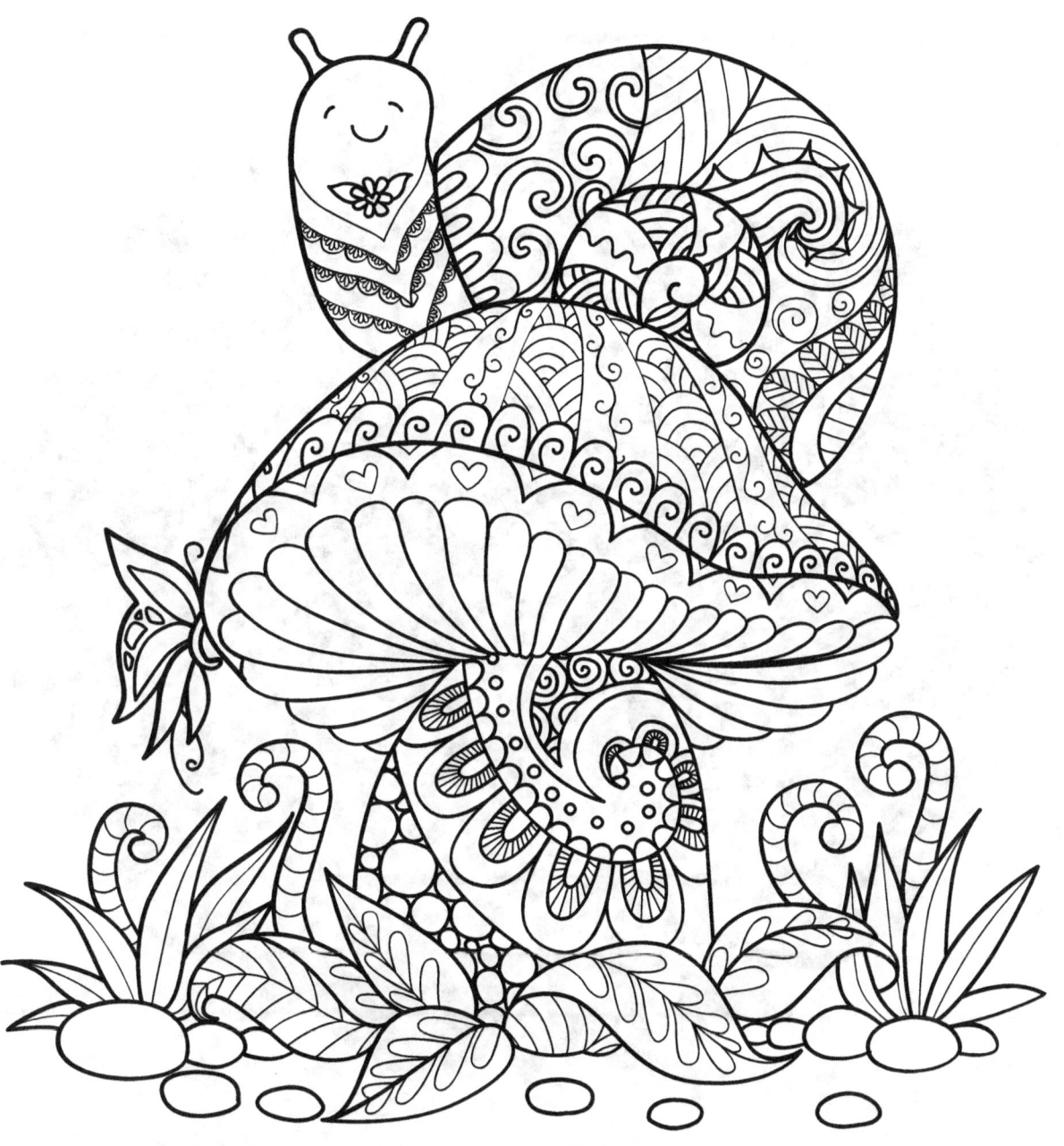

Triadic color: A bright and cheerful palette with bold primary colors.

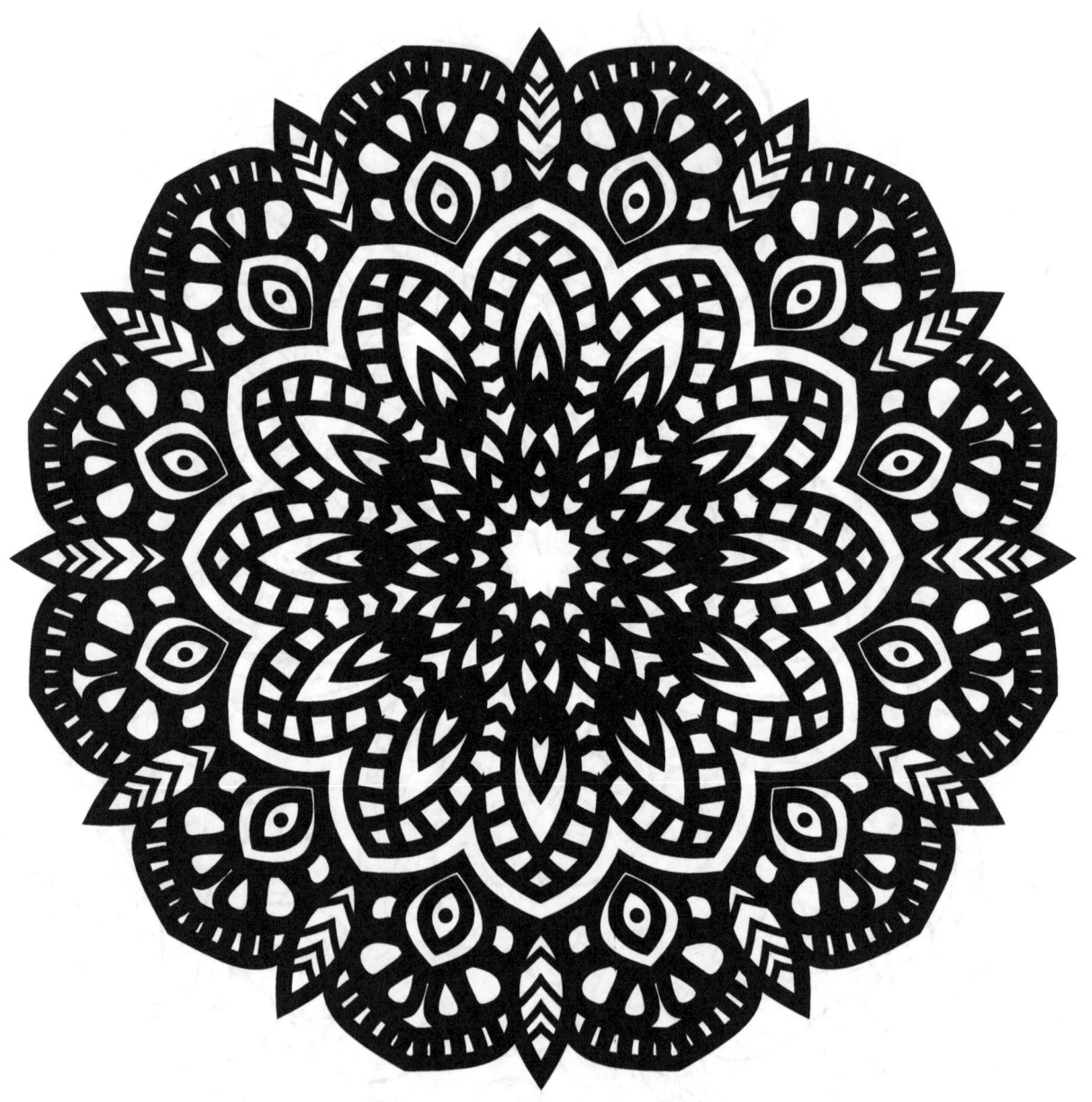

Think of birds and berries. Add dark brown of a branch, green of the feathers, pink of the berries with some lavender and cream.

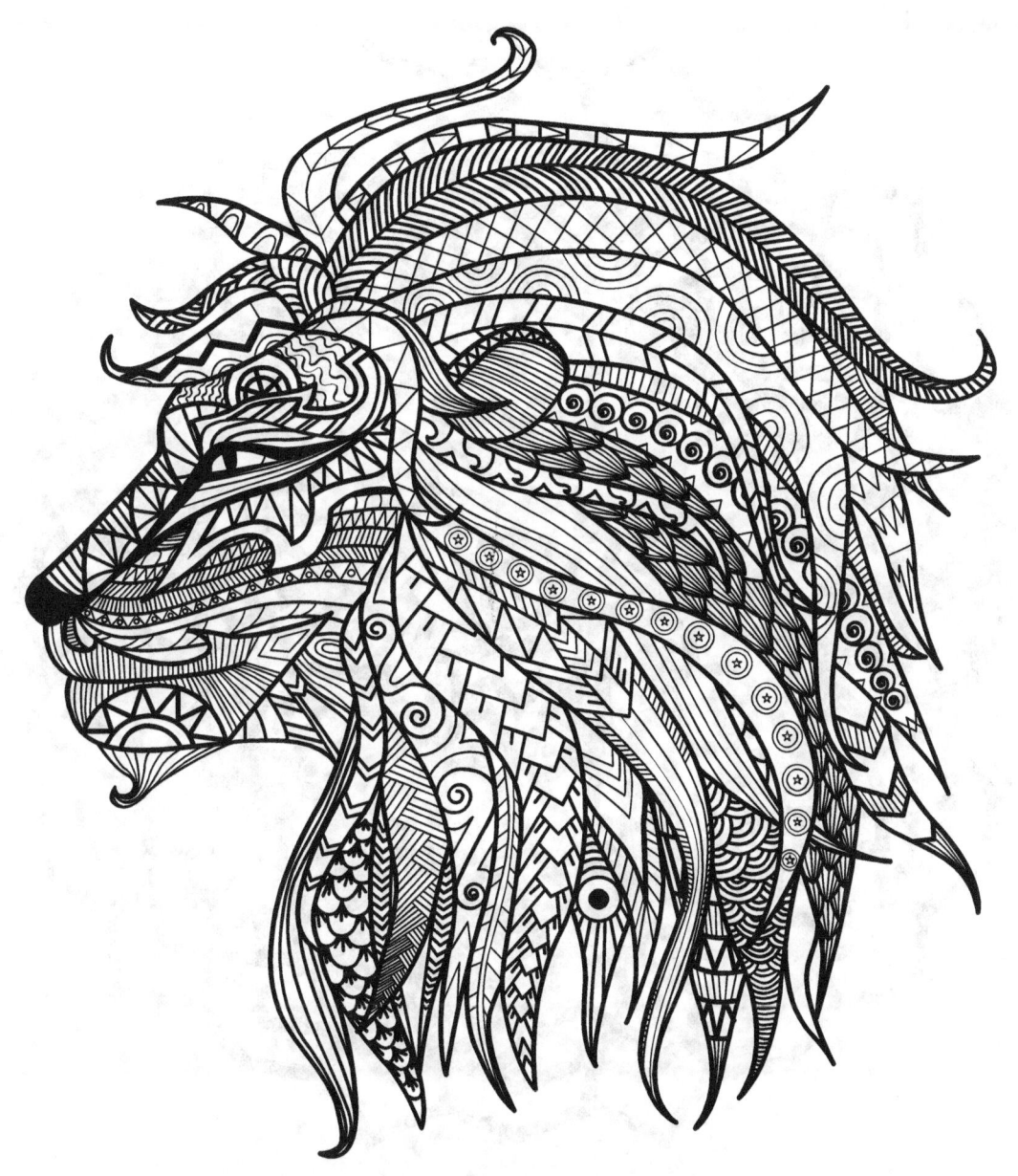

Pick a leaf that speaks to you and color it in using warm hues
that remind you of cozy fires and hot cocoa.

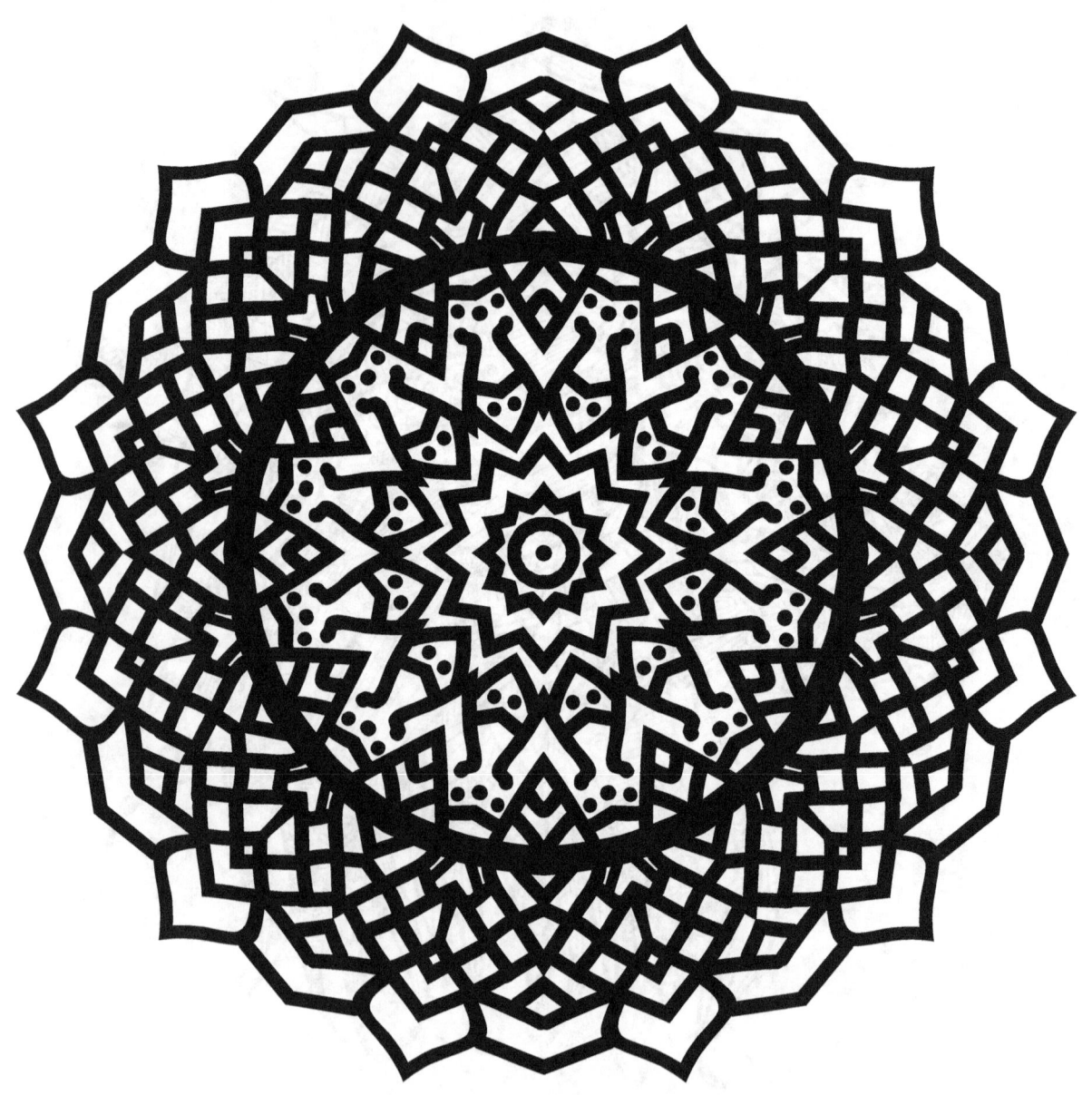

A color so tropical, you could feel the warm breeze. Add hot pink, bubble gum pink, yellow and bright green.

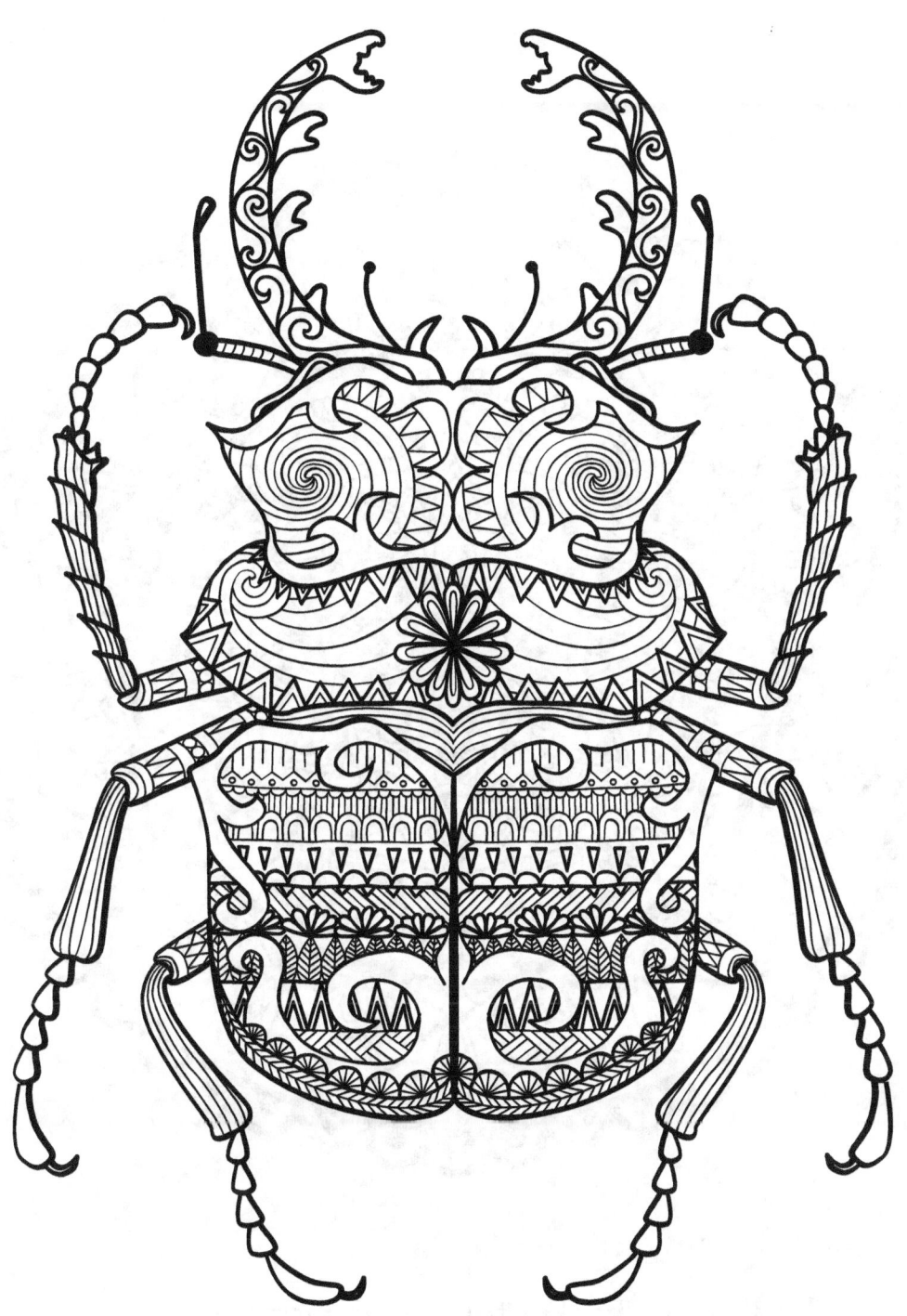

Fill in with the palette of moonlight. Pale yellow, cream white, moonlight blue, aero blue, absolute zero blue and sky grey.

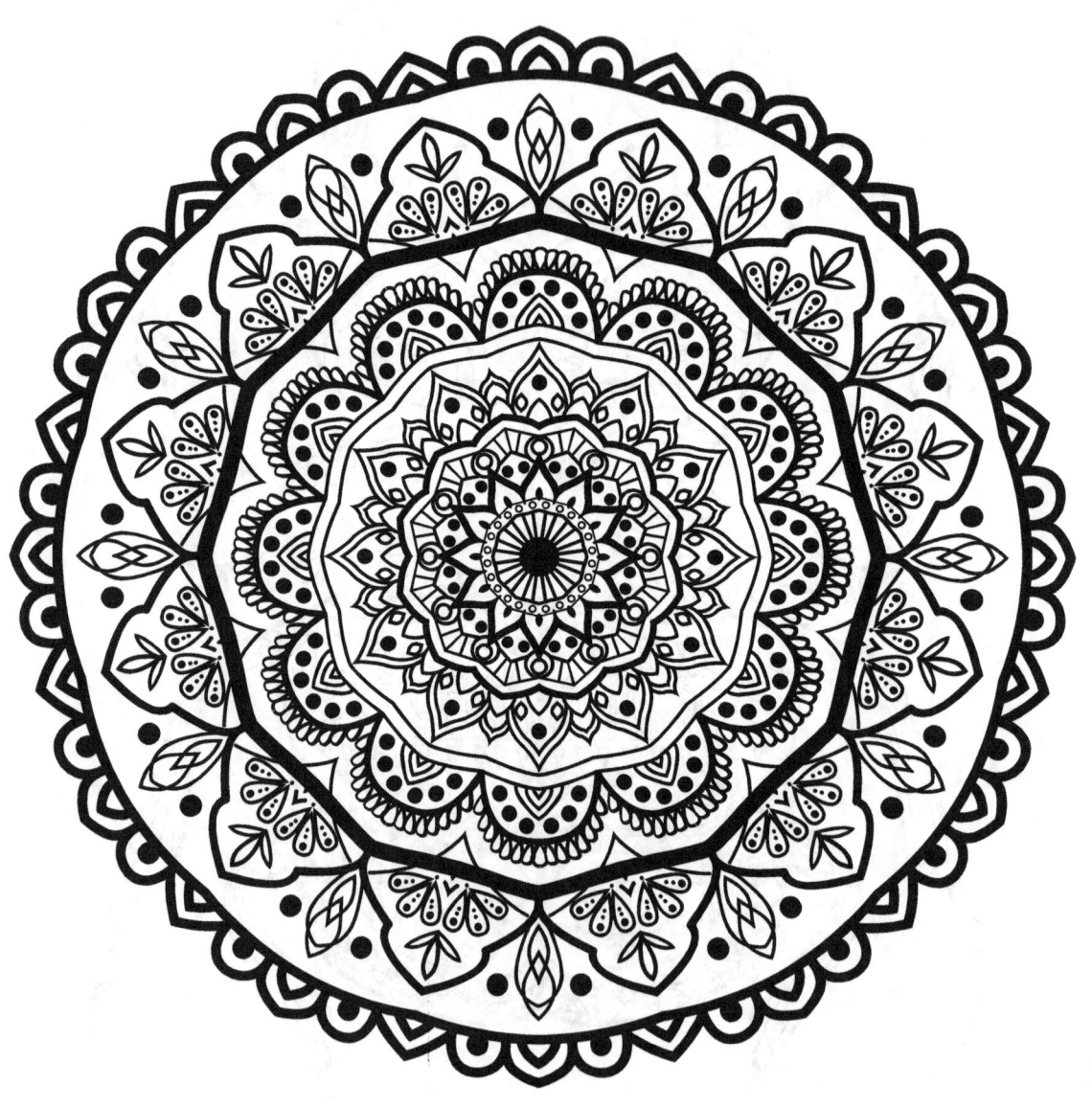

Think of a basket full of avocados, yellow
bell peppers and tomatoes.

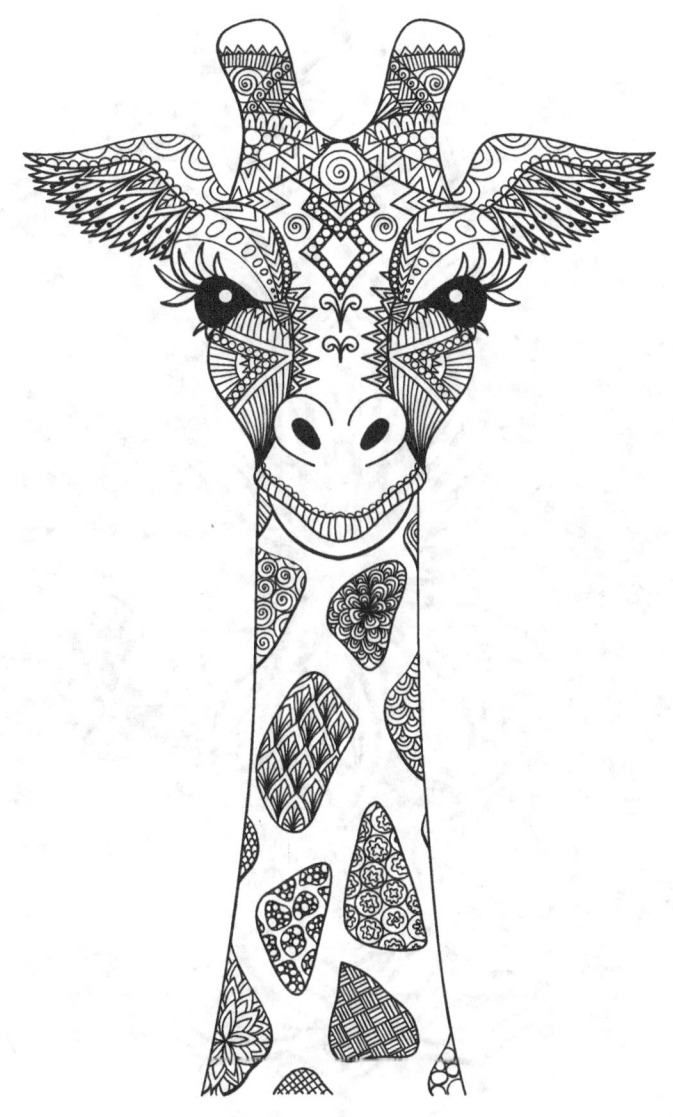

Pick a flower that resonates with you and color it in with bright, vibrant colors that remind you of sunshine and happiness.

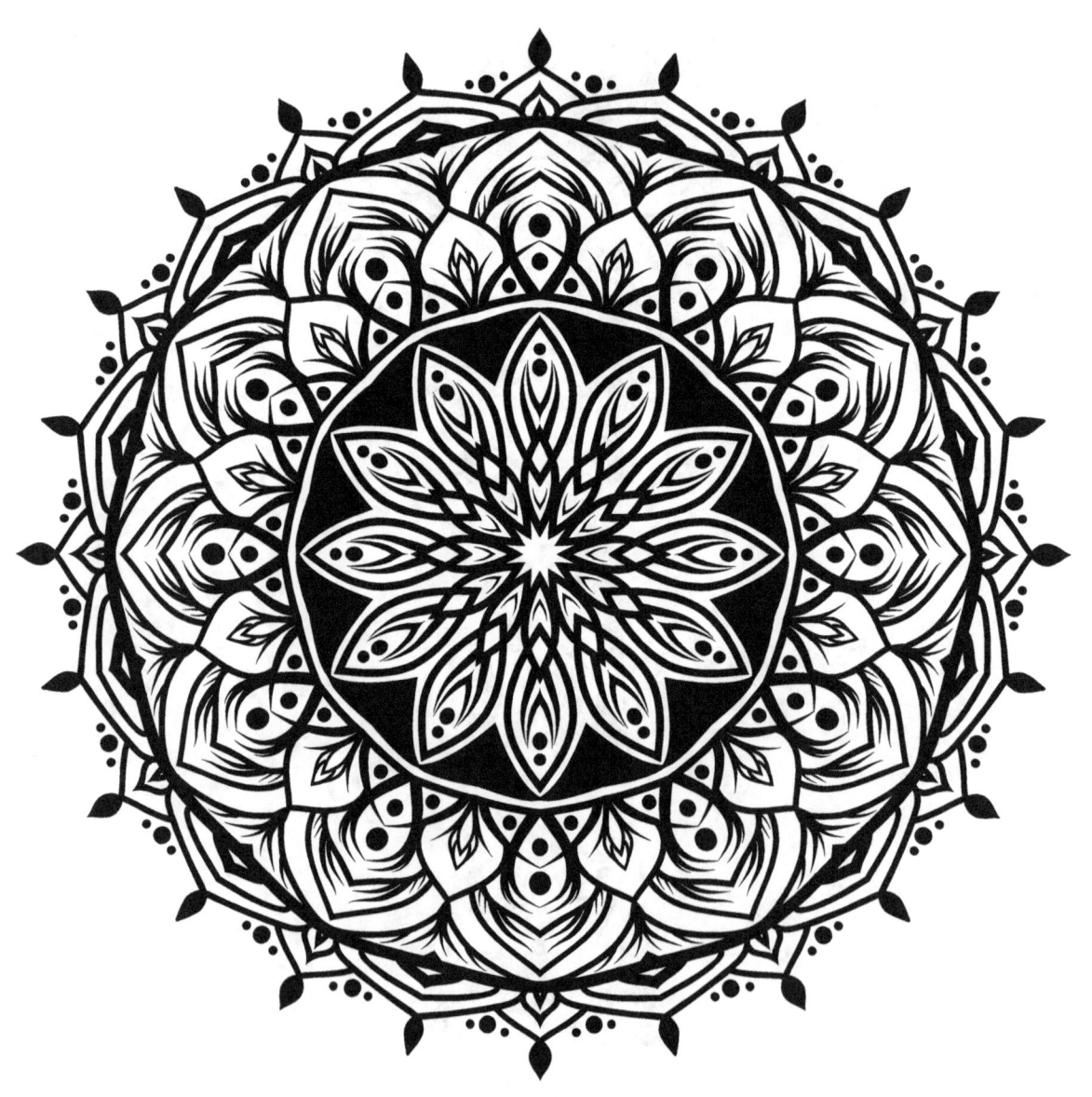

Think of macaroons. Color with pastel lavender, pinks and baby blue.

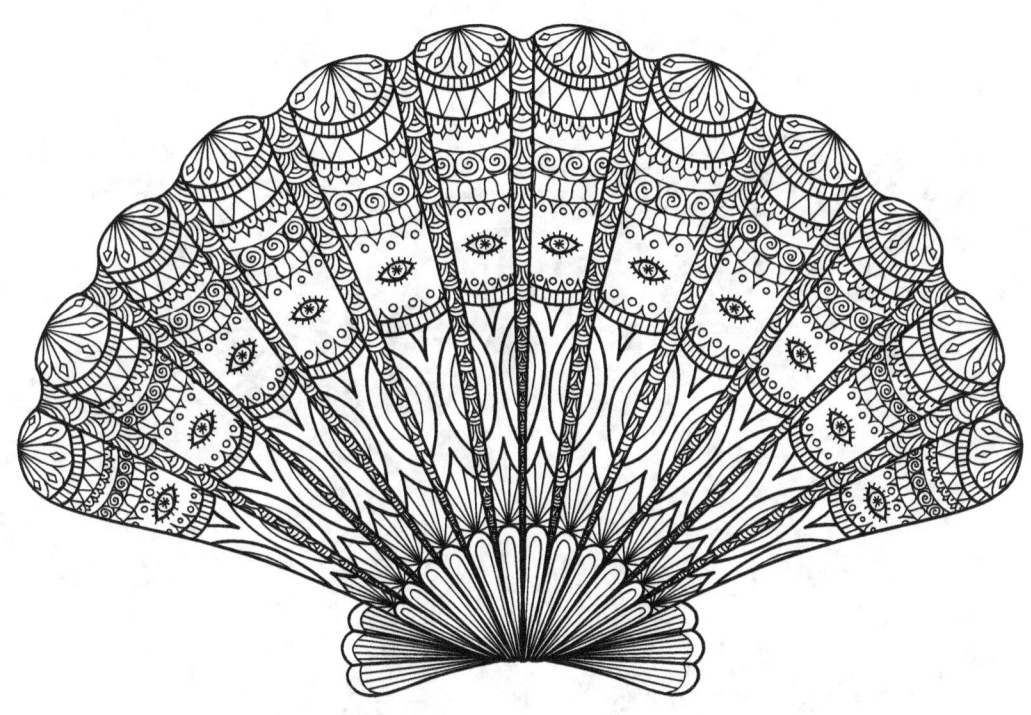

A nostalgic mix of 80s and 90s colors with a muted aesthetic.

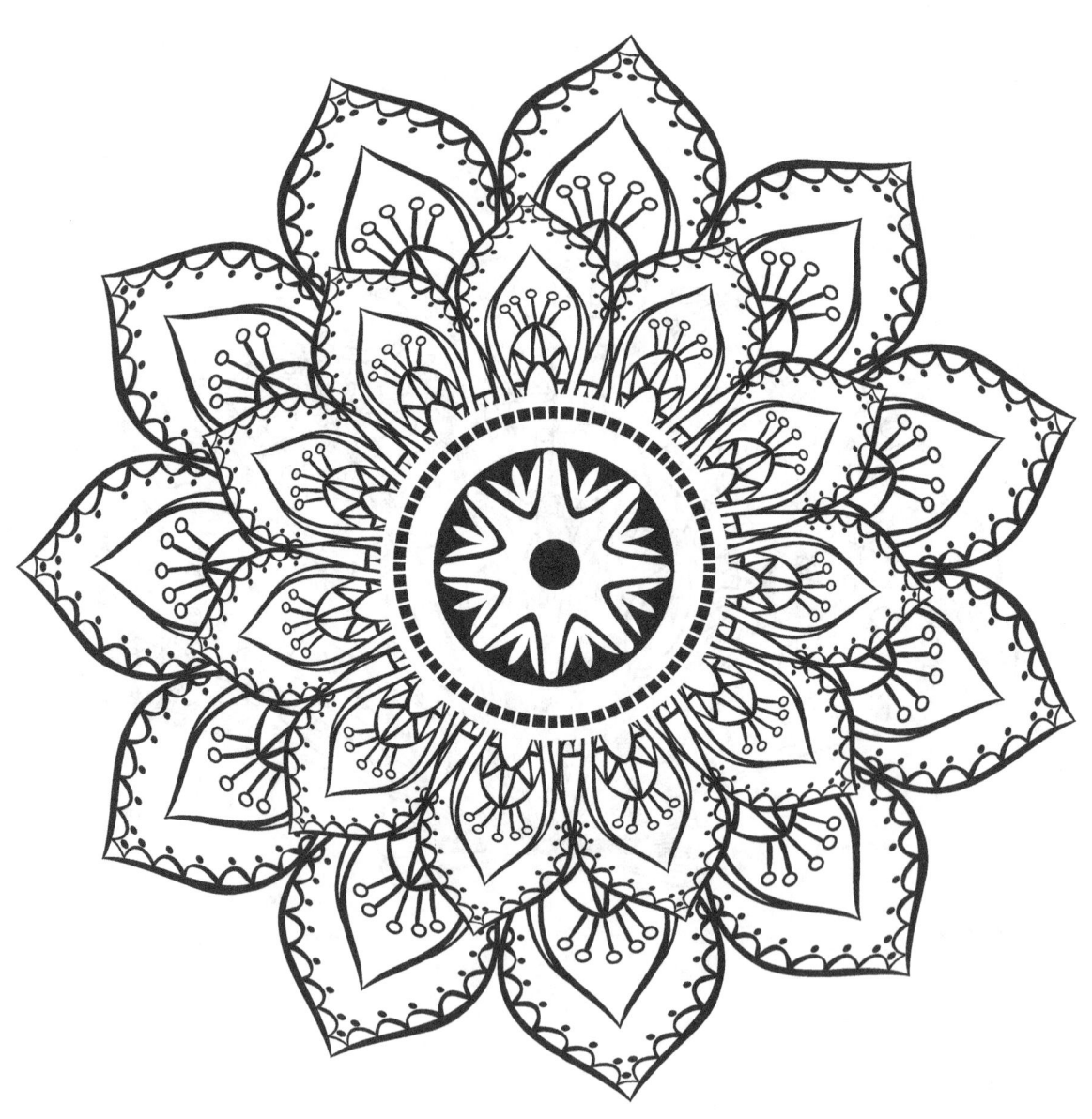

Galaxy. Add the colors from between interstellar dust and planets, add black, blue, silver, purple. Mix and make new colors.

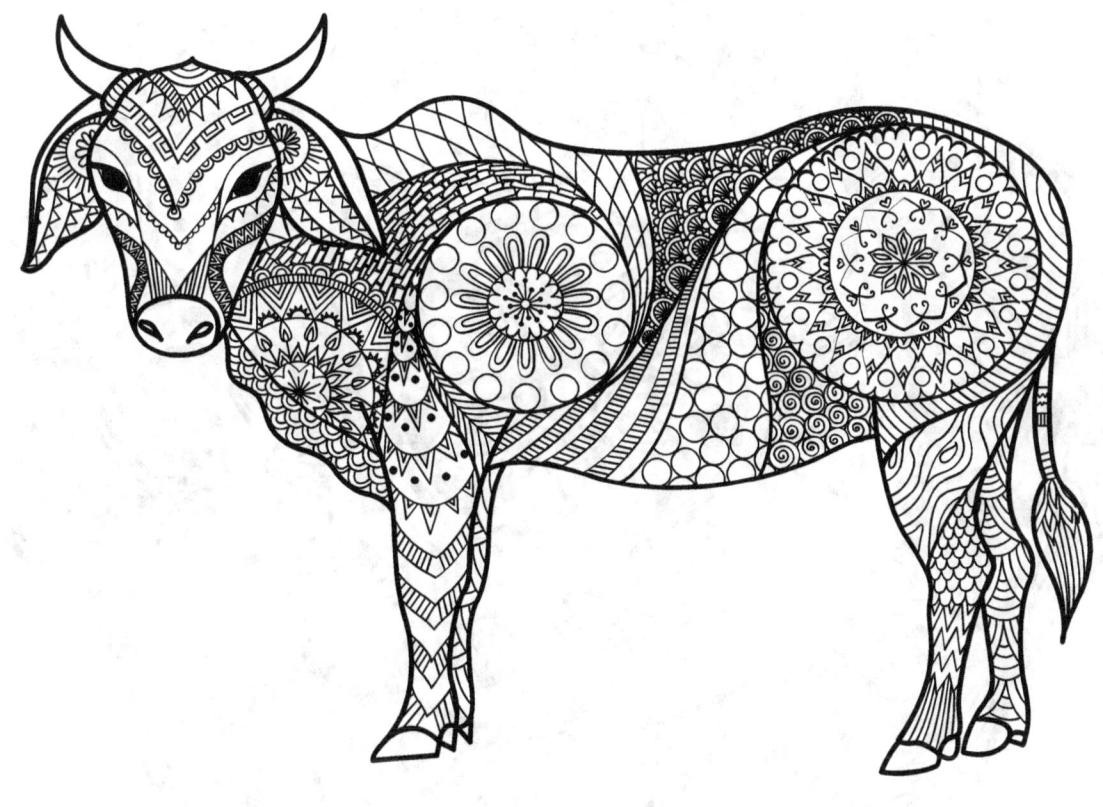

Think of a tutti Fruity palette. Add wild grape purple, tutti frutti, green myth and sculpture grey.

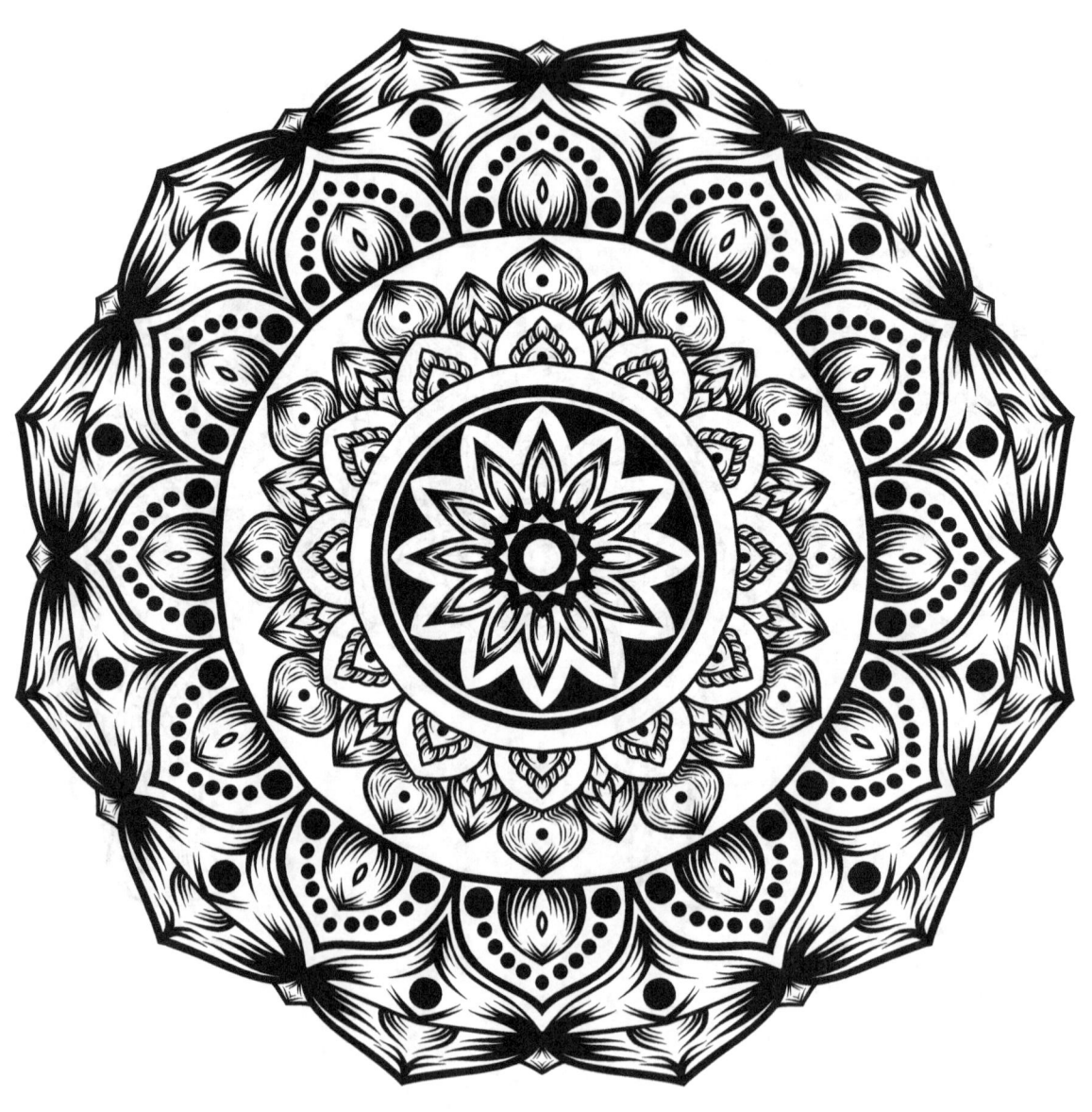

Butterflies comes in a variety of color. Choose your favorite and use the palette here.

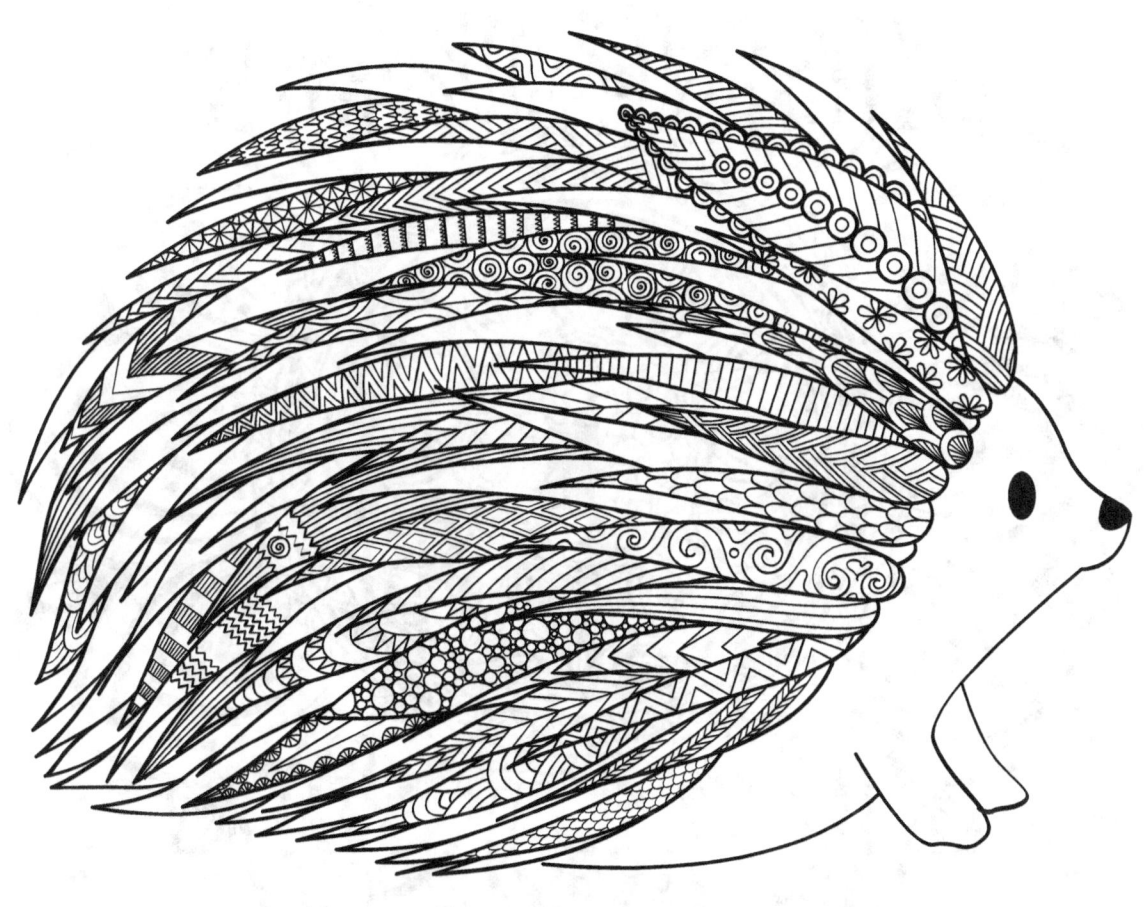

Kawaii Pastel: Sweet and innocent colors with a childlike charm.

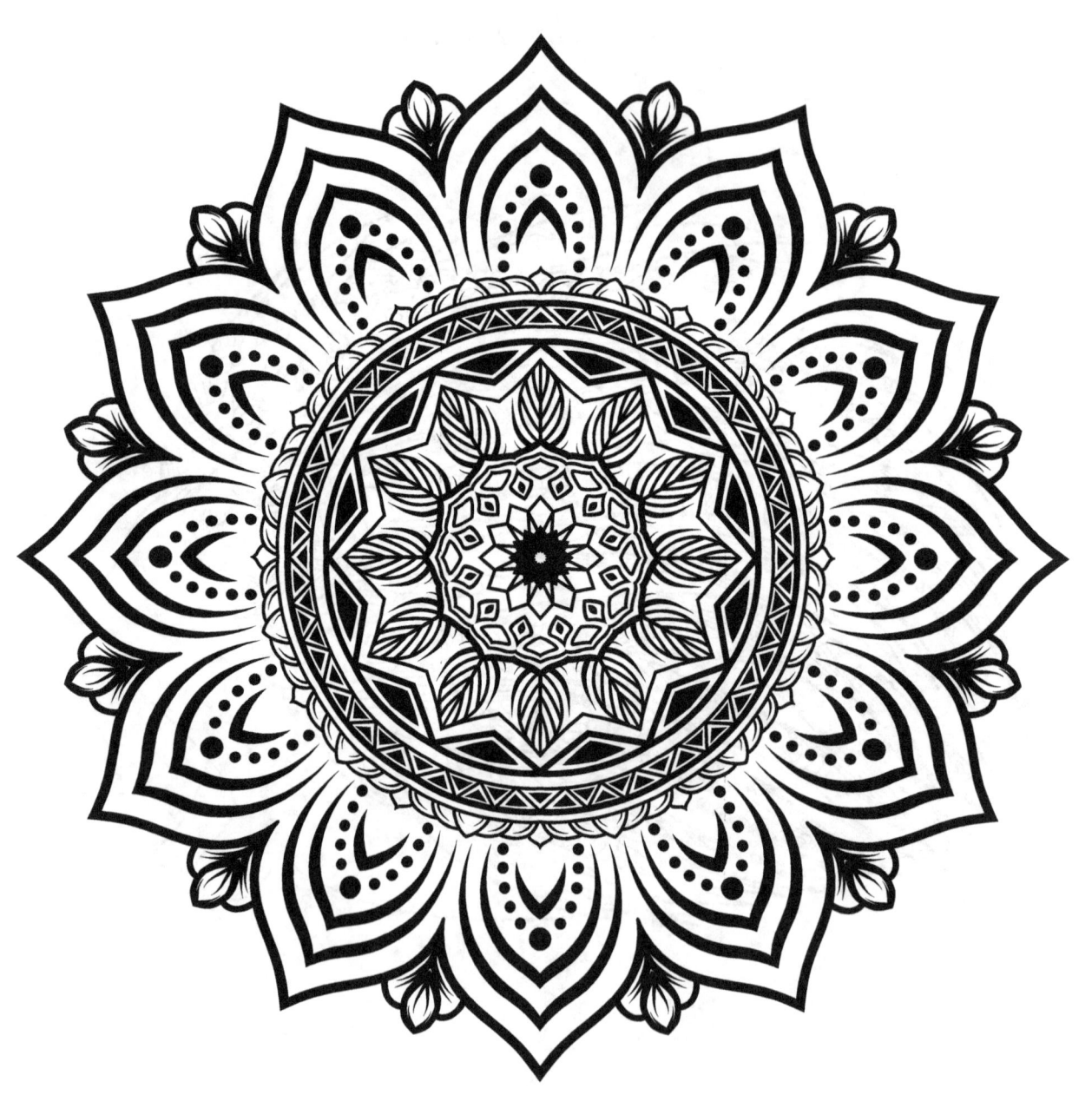

Think of the beige and grey tones you see in the collection of seashells.

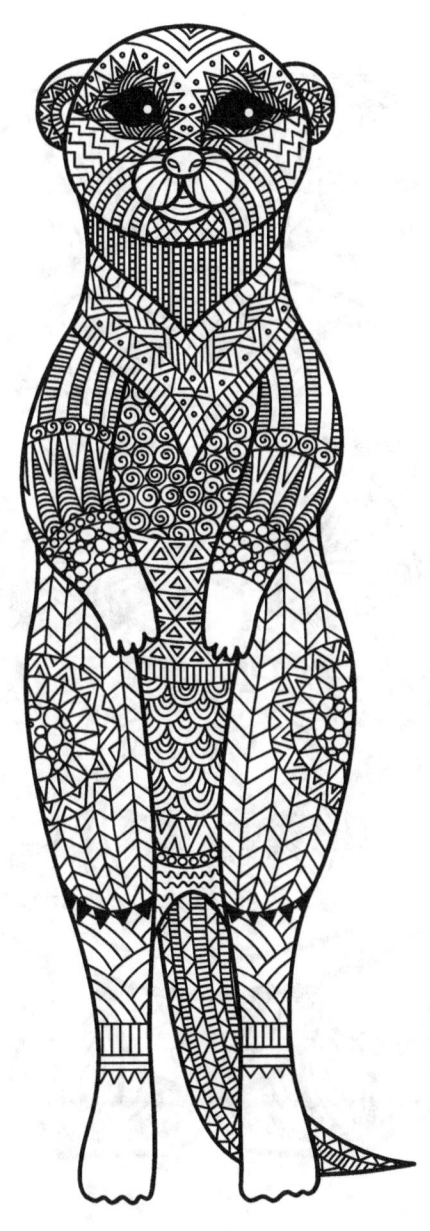

Mix pinks with violets. Add Chinese violet, cinnamon satin, coffee and chili red

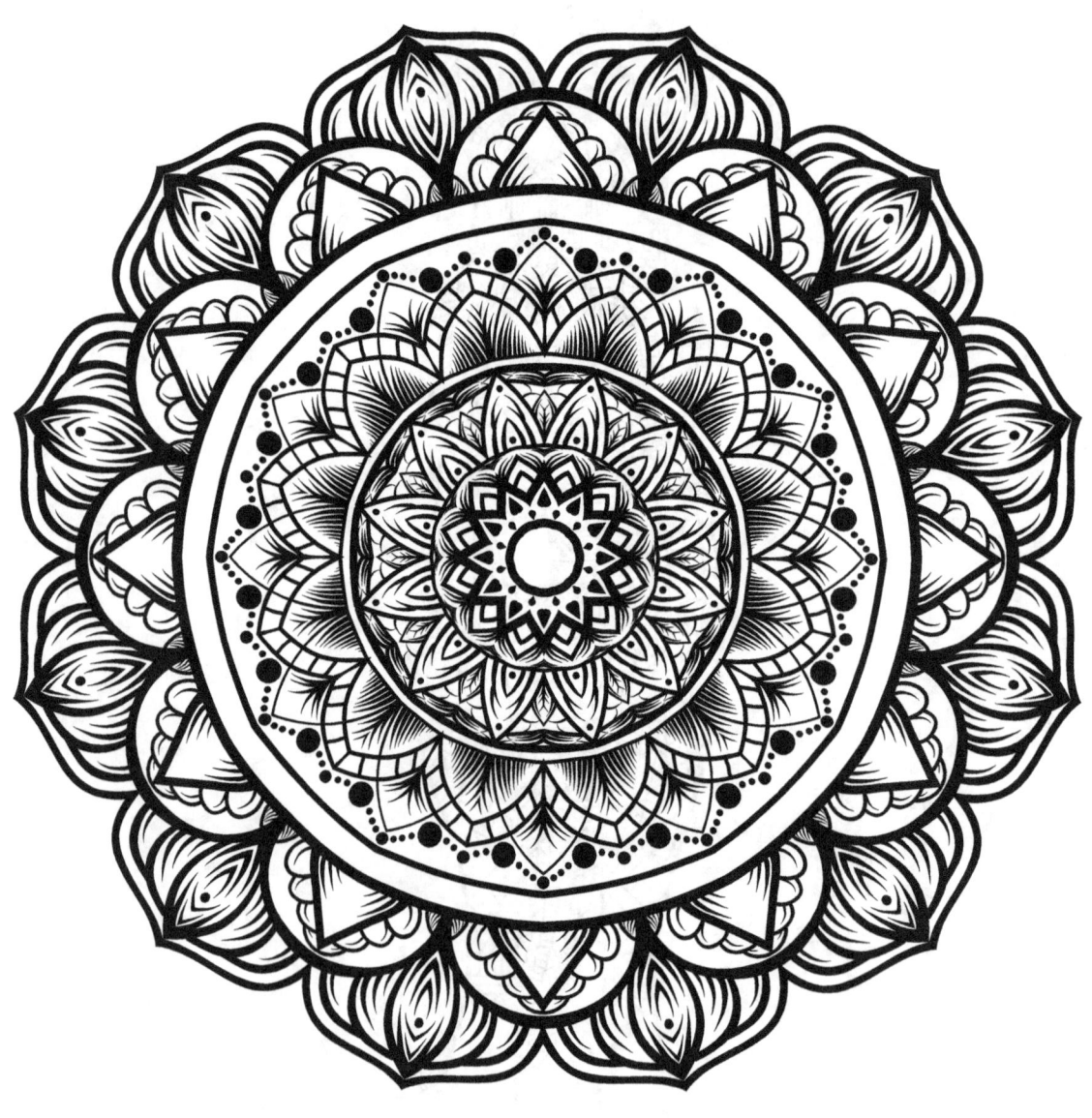

Insects come in all colors. Think of one and paint it here.

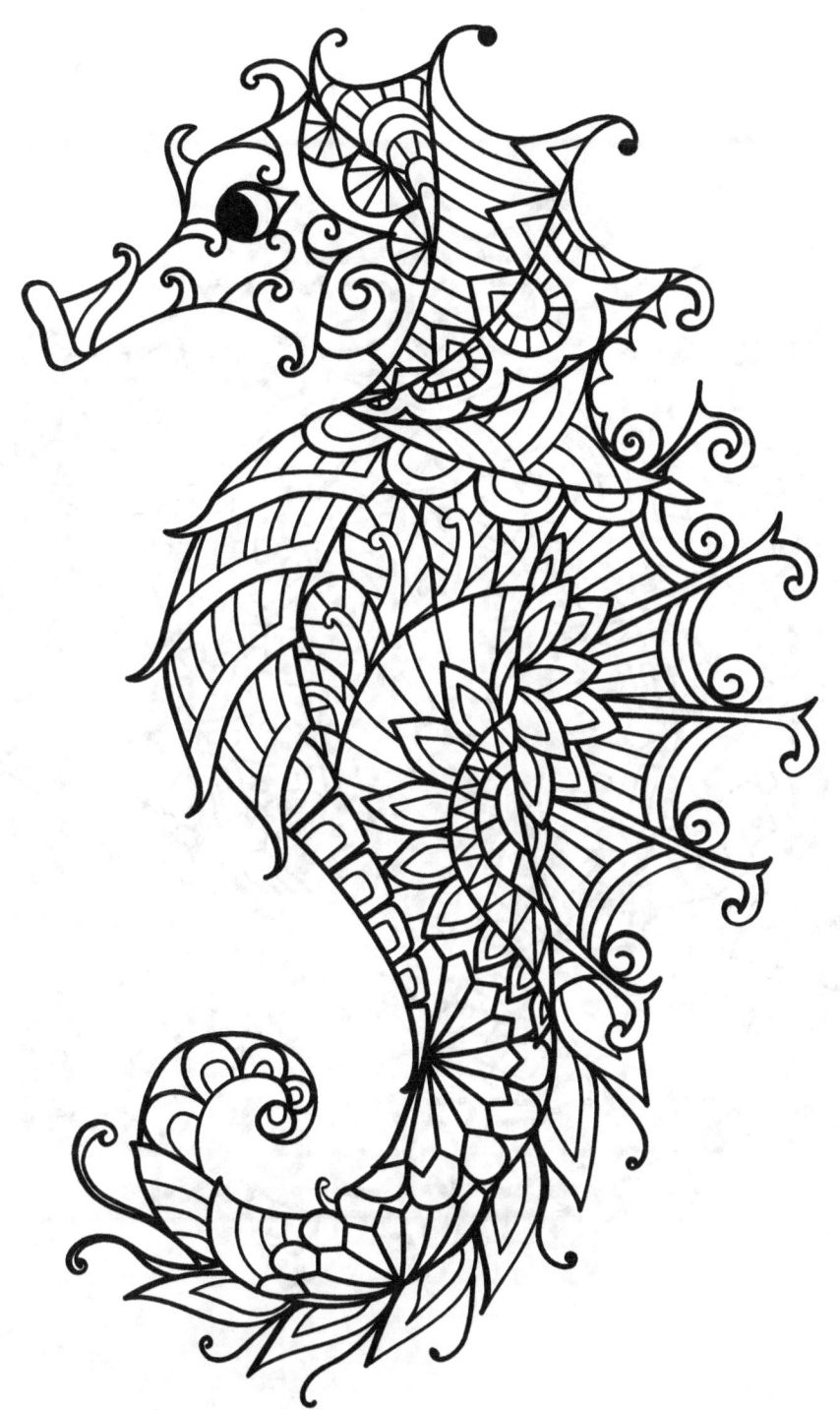

Lofi: Soft and dreamy colors with a faded quality.

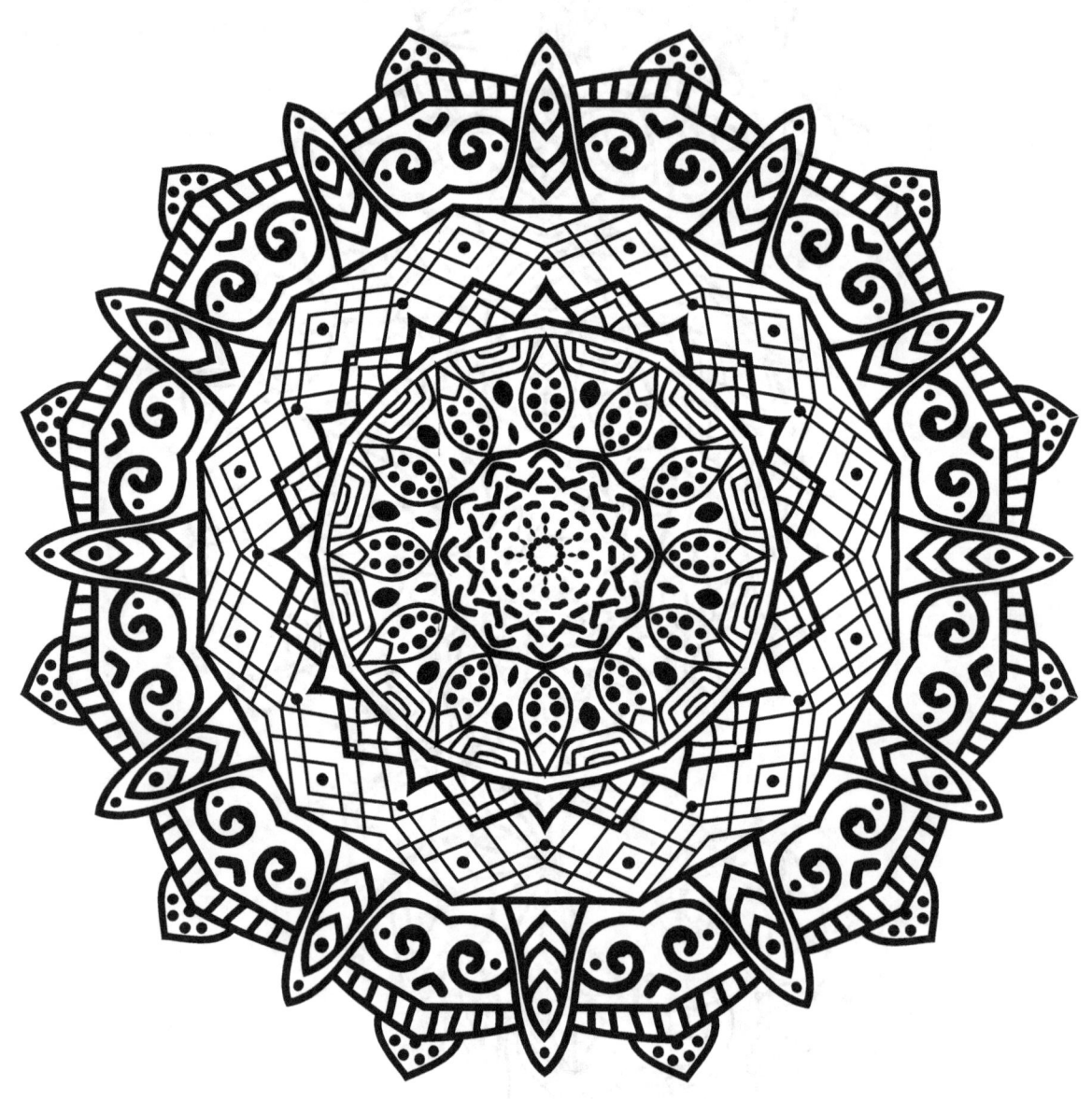

Colors of Halloween. Use the many shades of orange, blacks and brown.

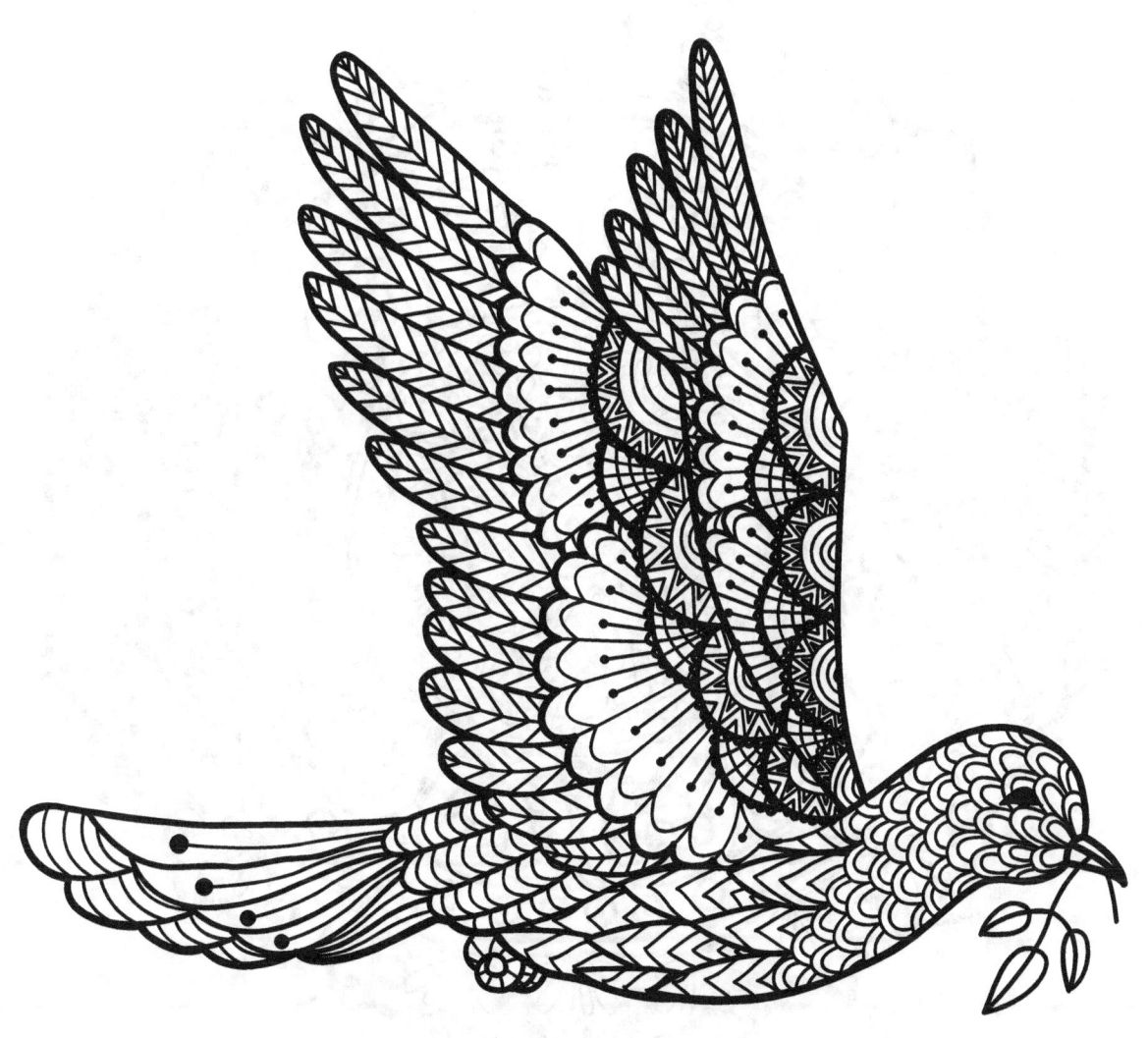

Go Charcoal. Use Charcoal to fill this mandala.

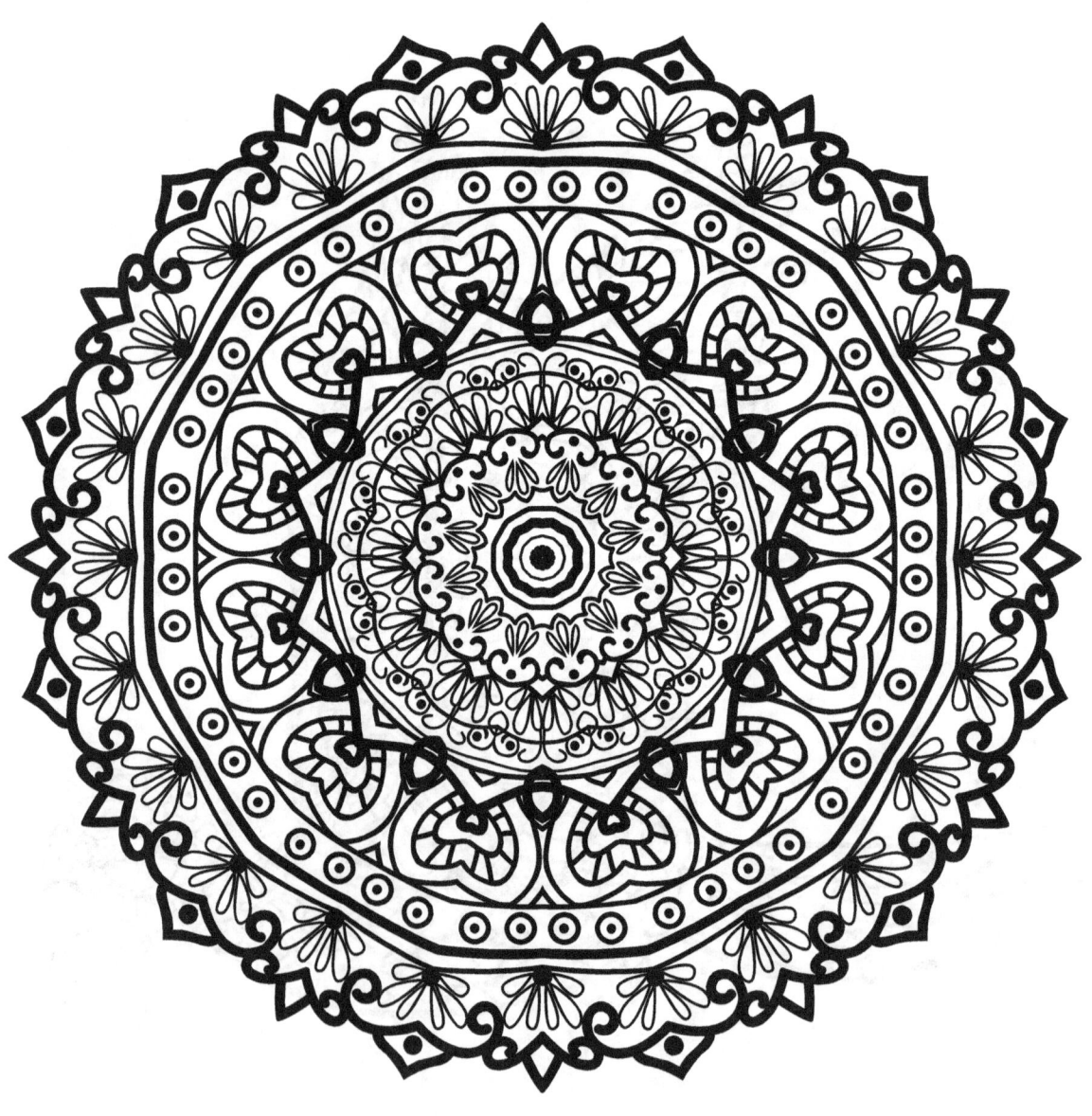

Plenty of fish in the ocean. Think of your favorite or image
search, then use its colors here.

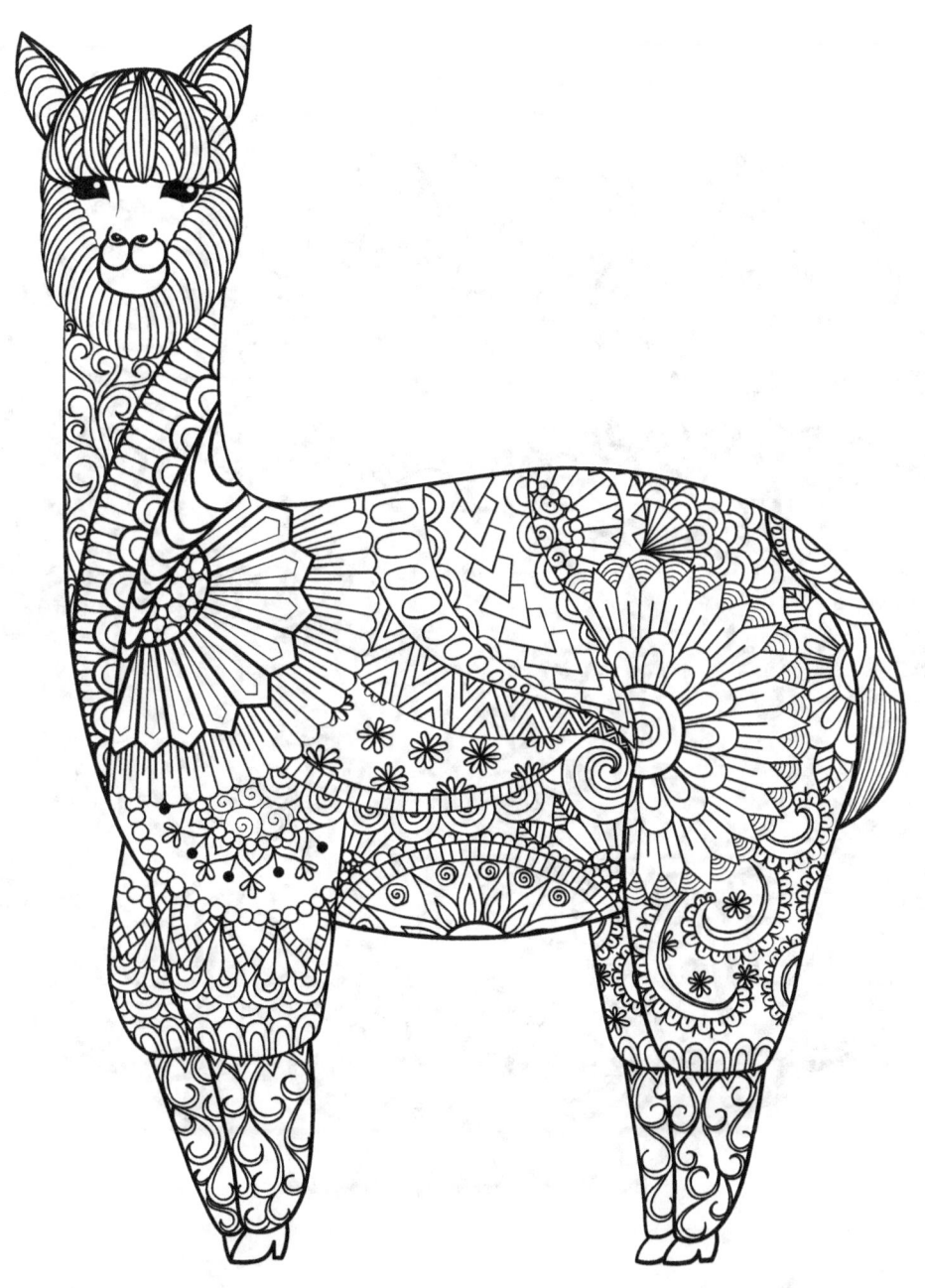

Color it with the choice of your favorite artist's piece.

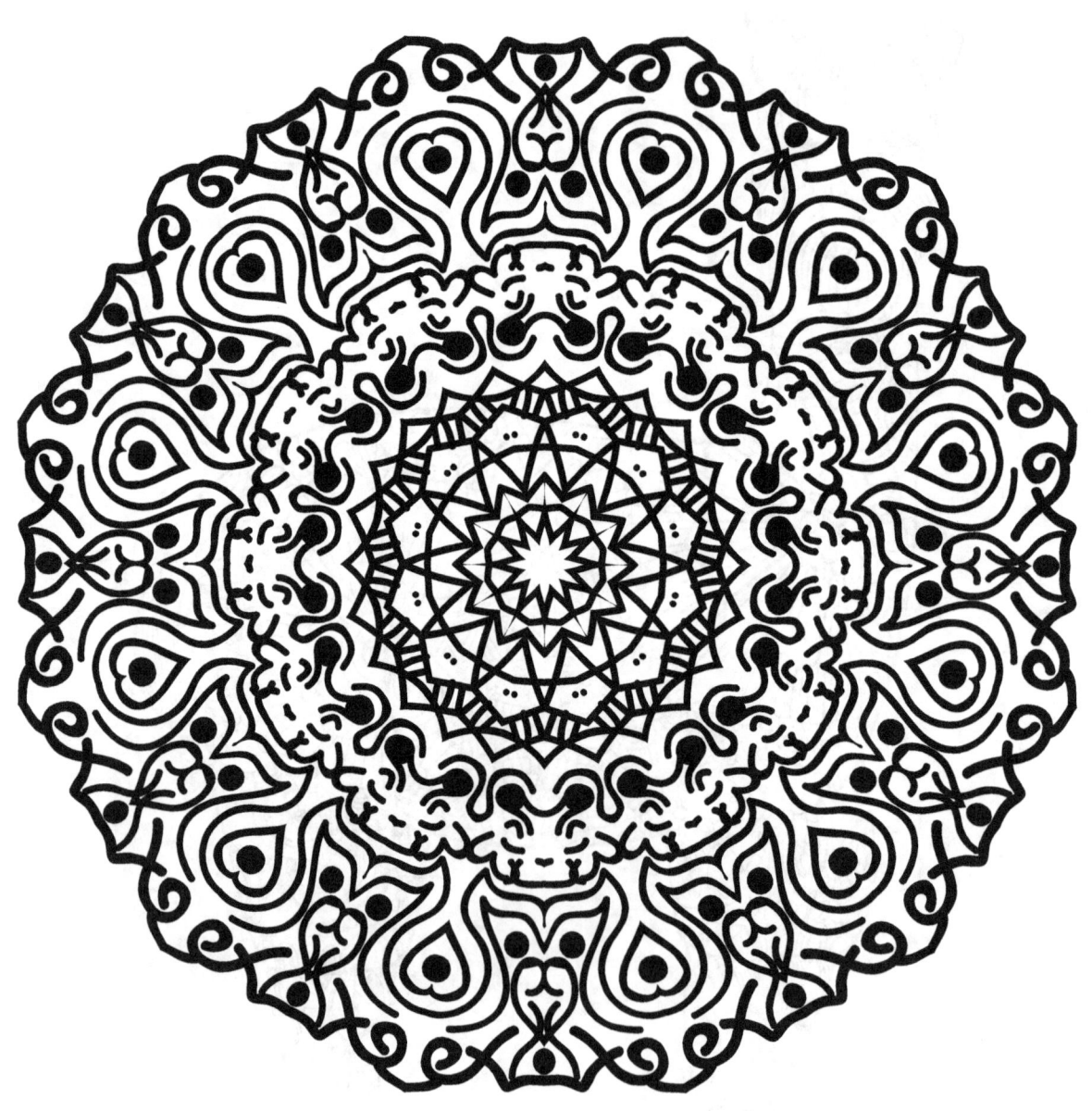

Choose your pet's colors. Color it with the color of your pet with any 2 contrasting color of your choice.

Use the colors of your favorite animated character.

Use colors of your 3 favorite drinks.

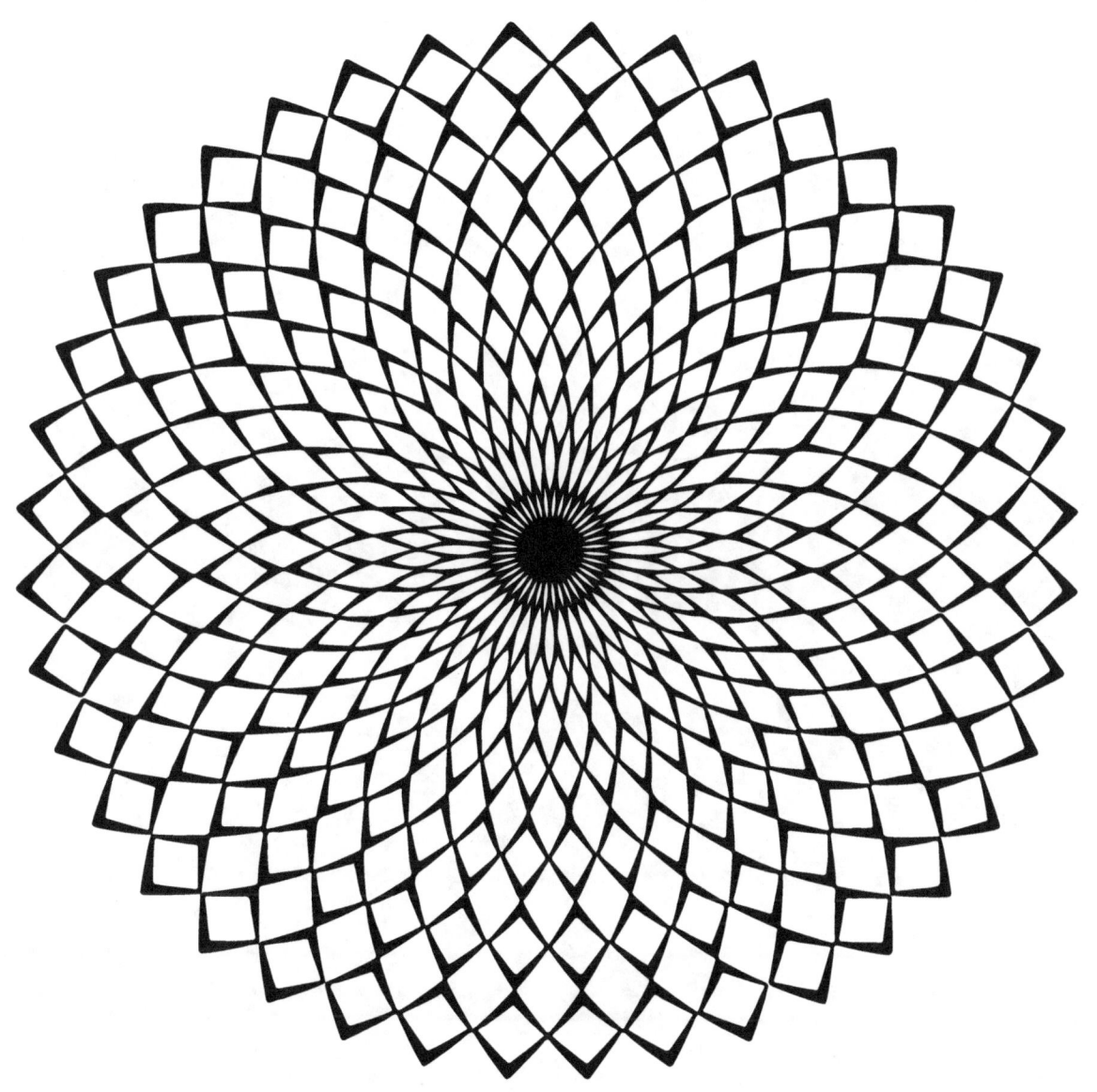

Opal. Crème, light green and French blue.

Think of all that glitters. Gold, diamonds. Color this page like a treasure chest full of rubies, sapphire, and emerald.

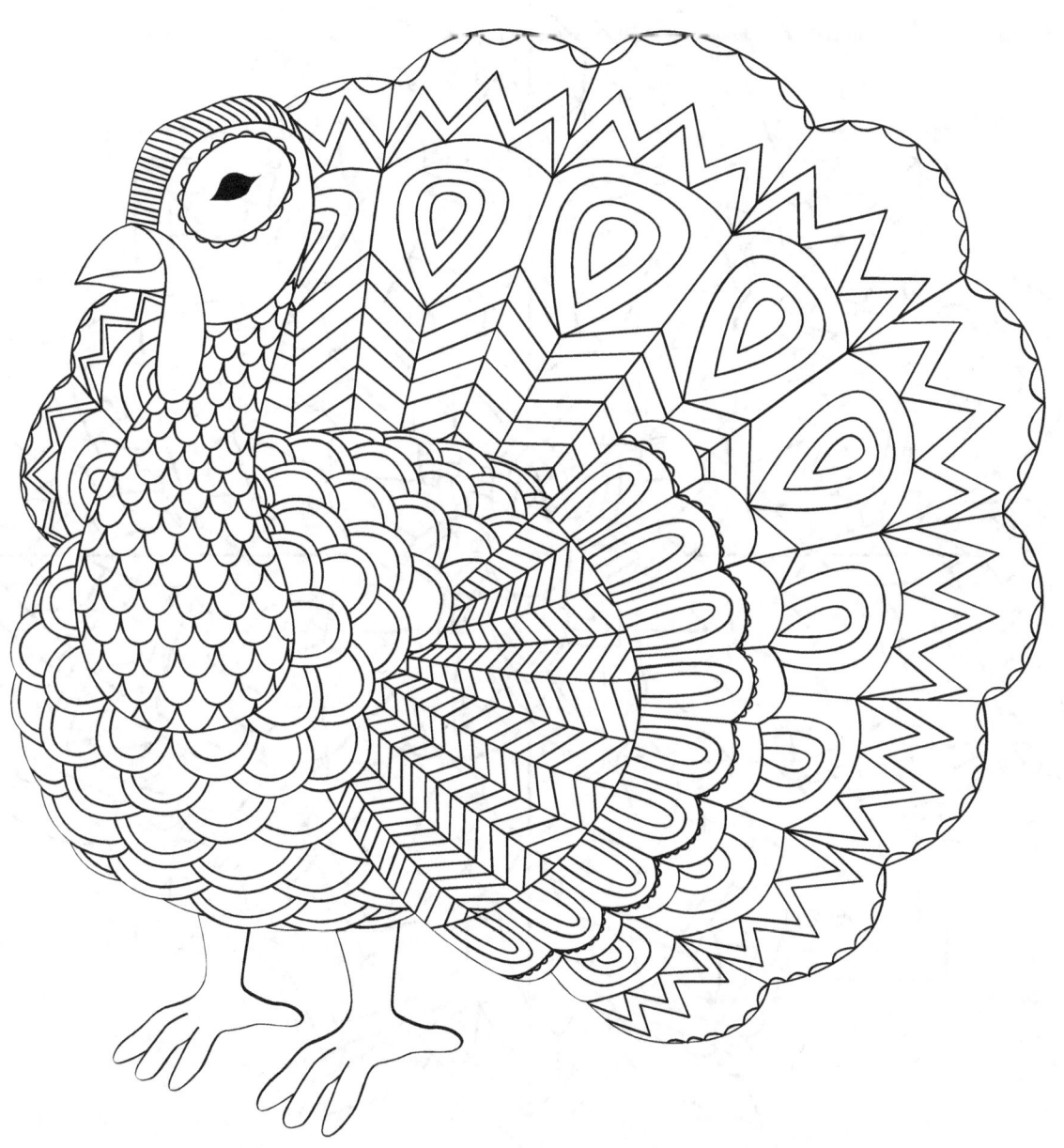

Color it with the theme of an event you are passionate about.

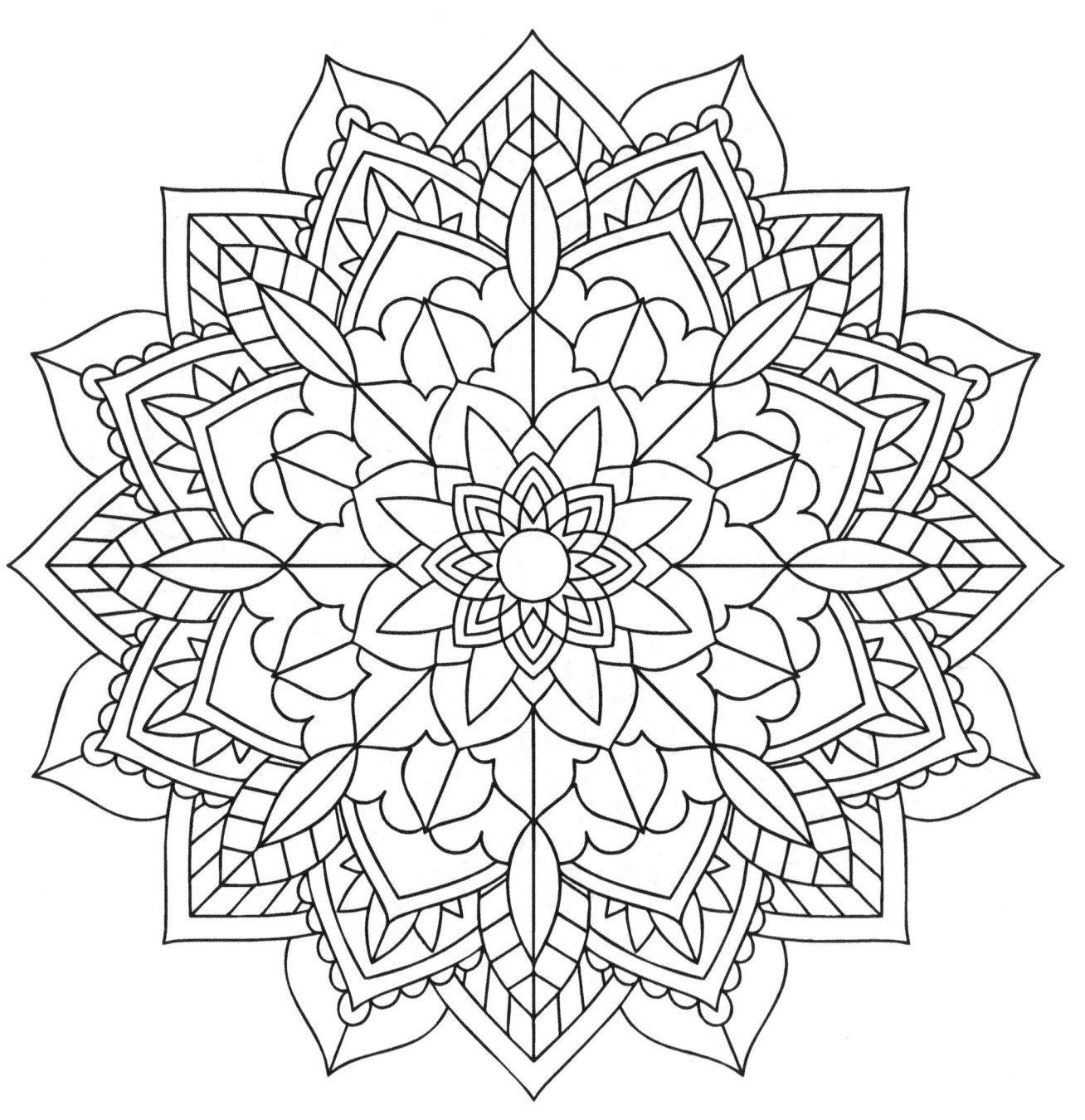

Colors of rainbows.

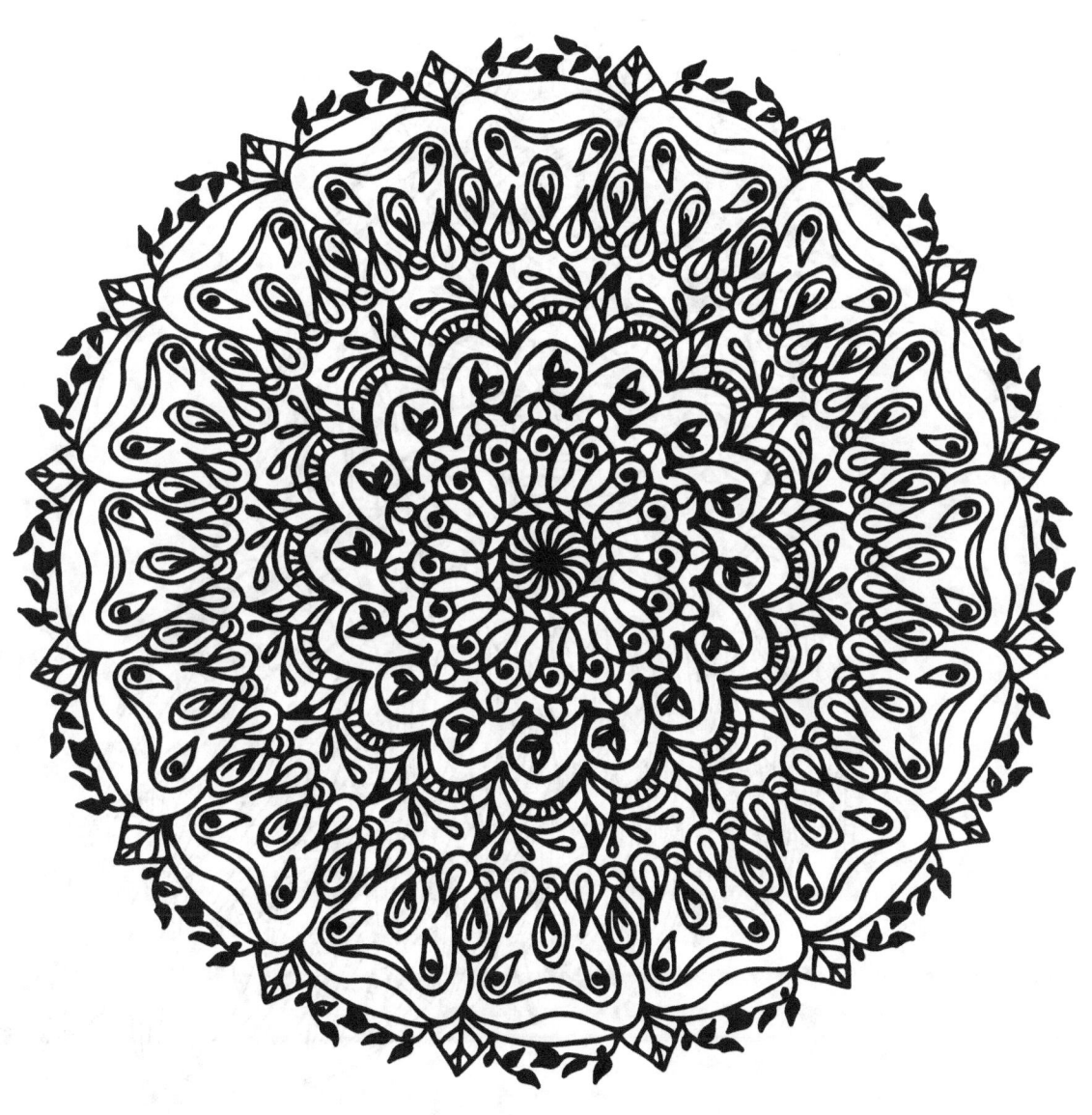

Cotton candy and unicorns.

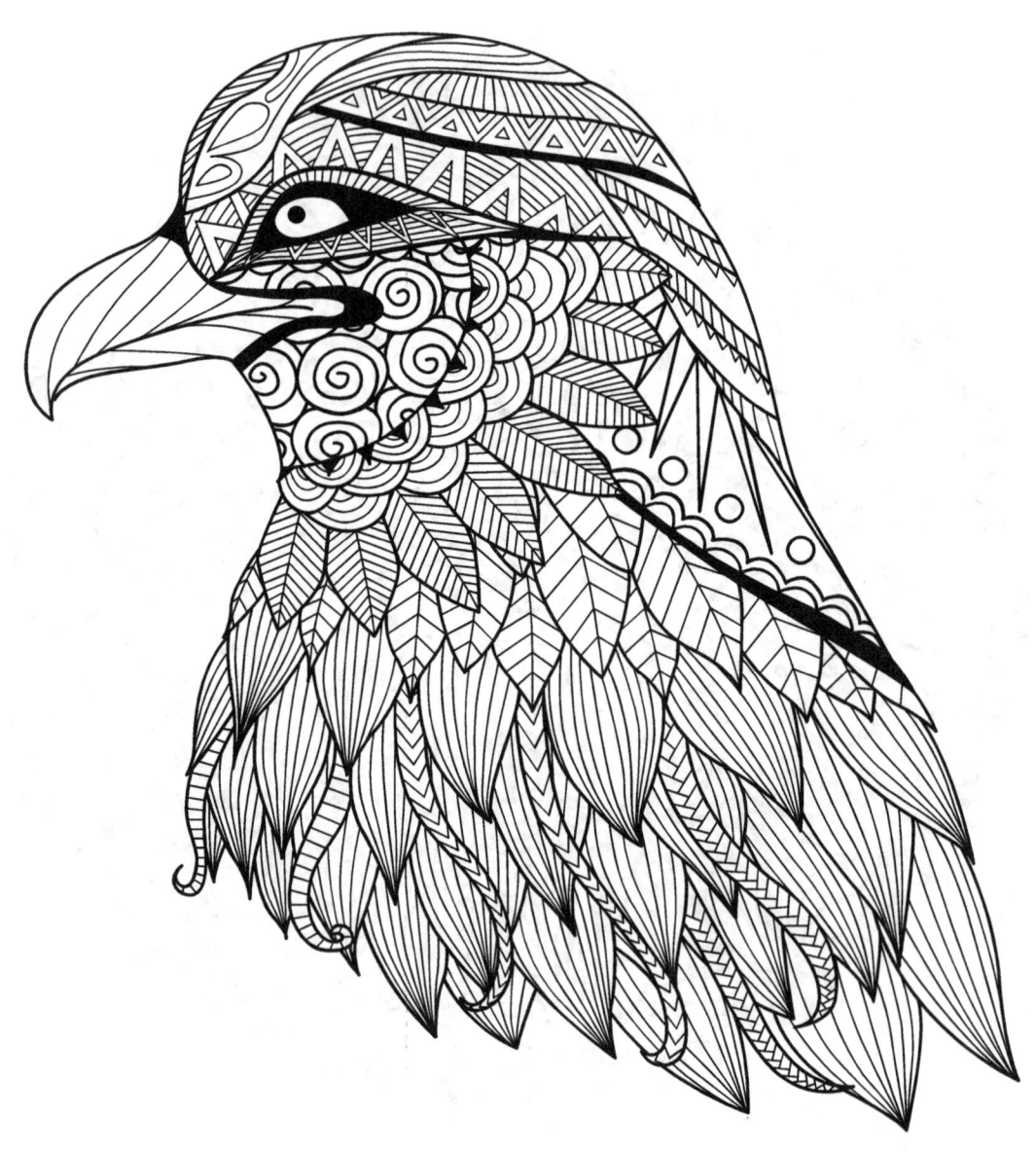

Whites have shades. Surprise yourself by filling in with ivory white, frost, bone white and pearl white.

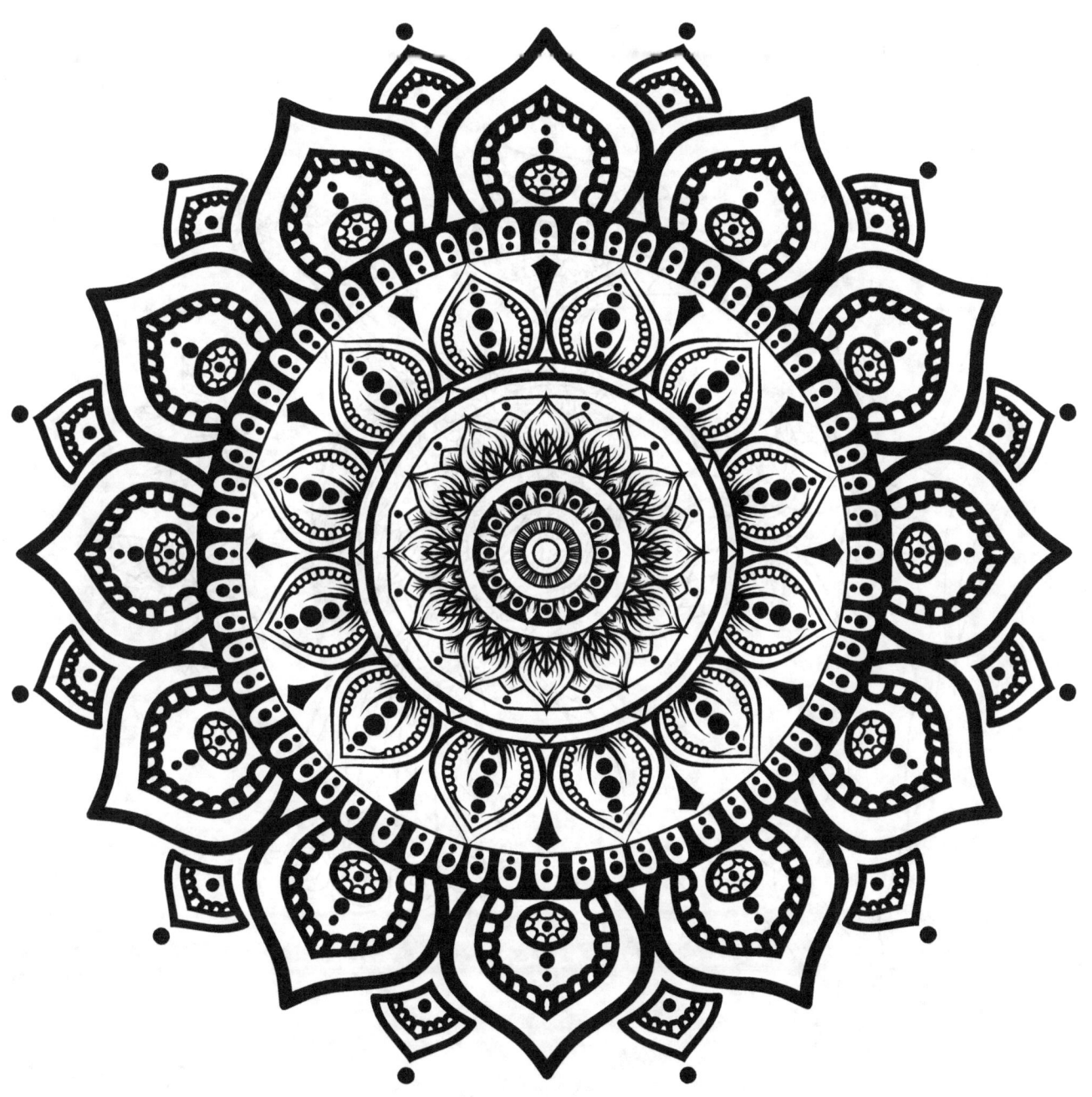

From Golden brown hues to checkered cheetah. Fill this page with the colors of savannahs.

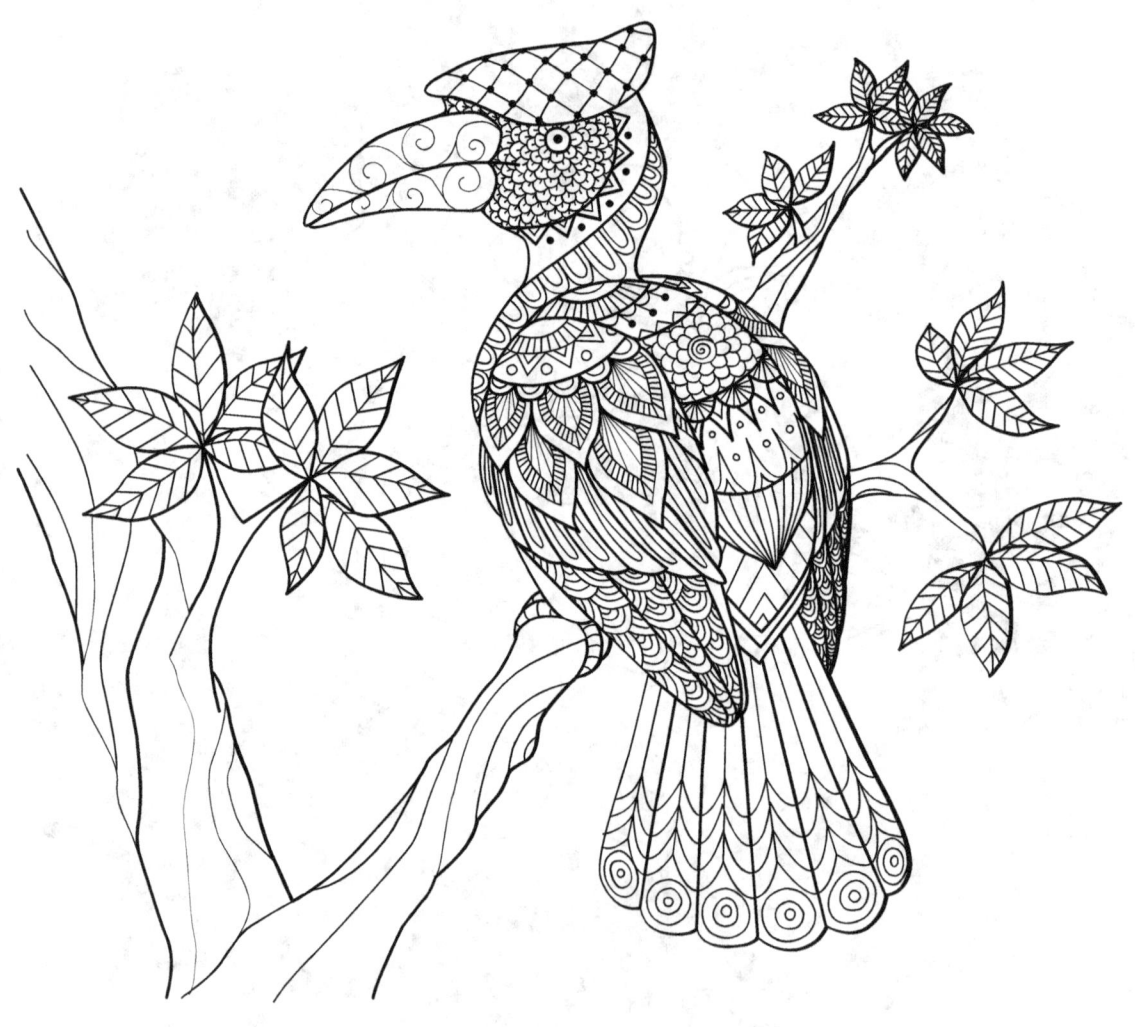

Green is subtle and calm, contrast with orange to add vibrancy.

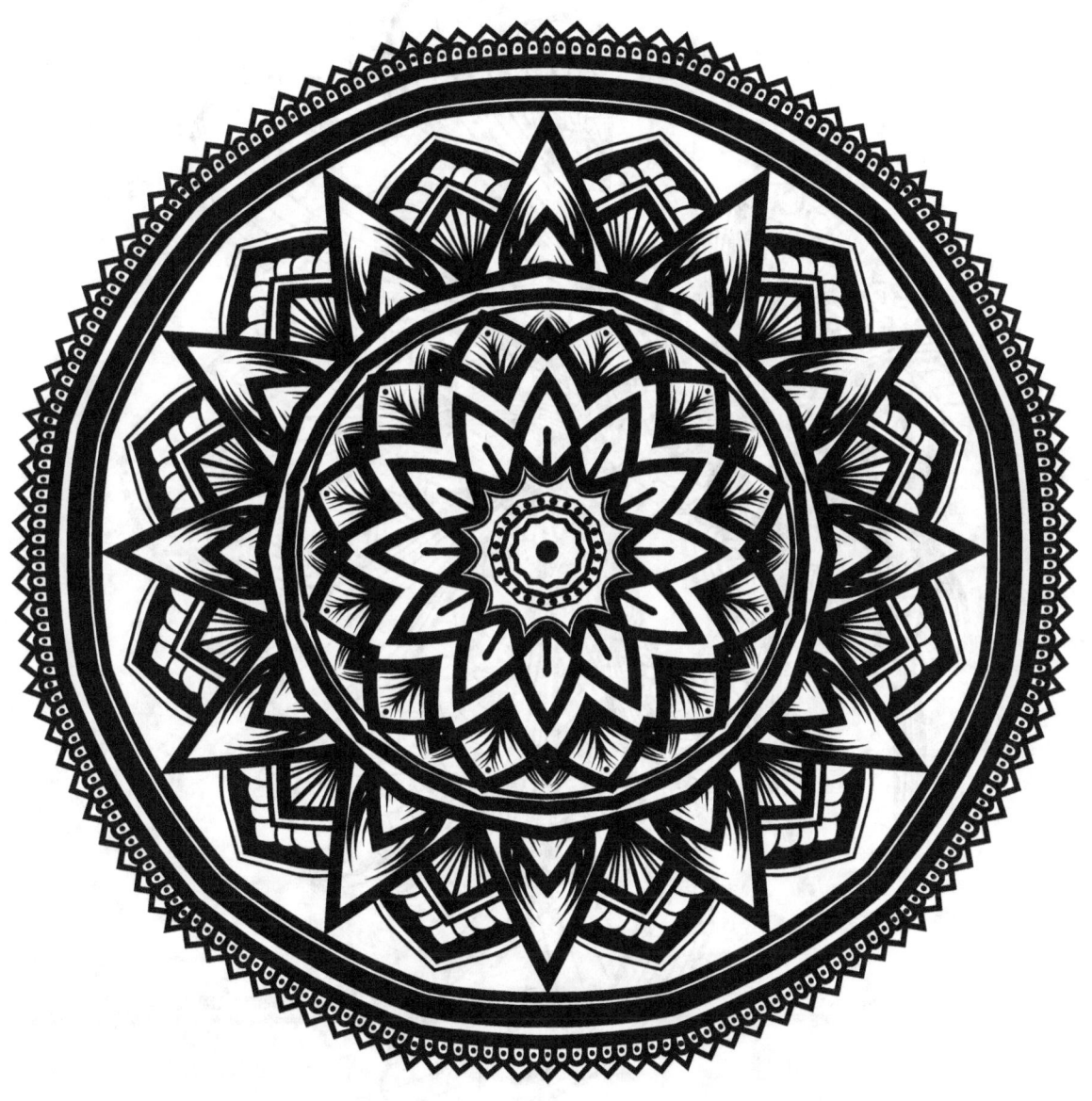

Color this page with the flag of the country you
are currently residing in!

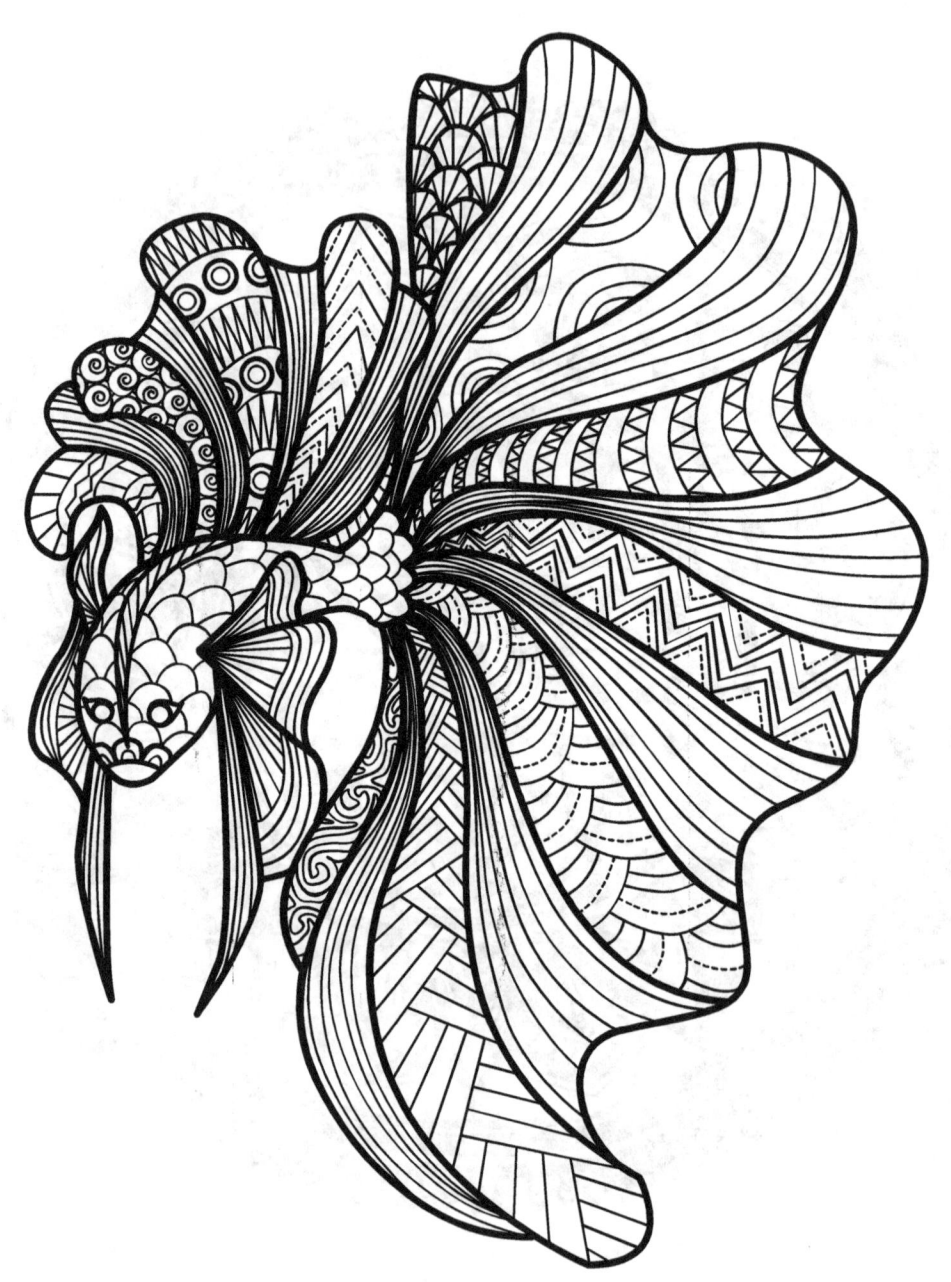

Cyberpunk: Bright, high-tech colors with an industrial feel.

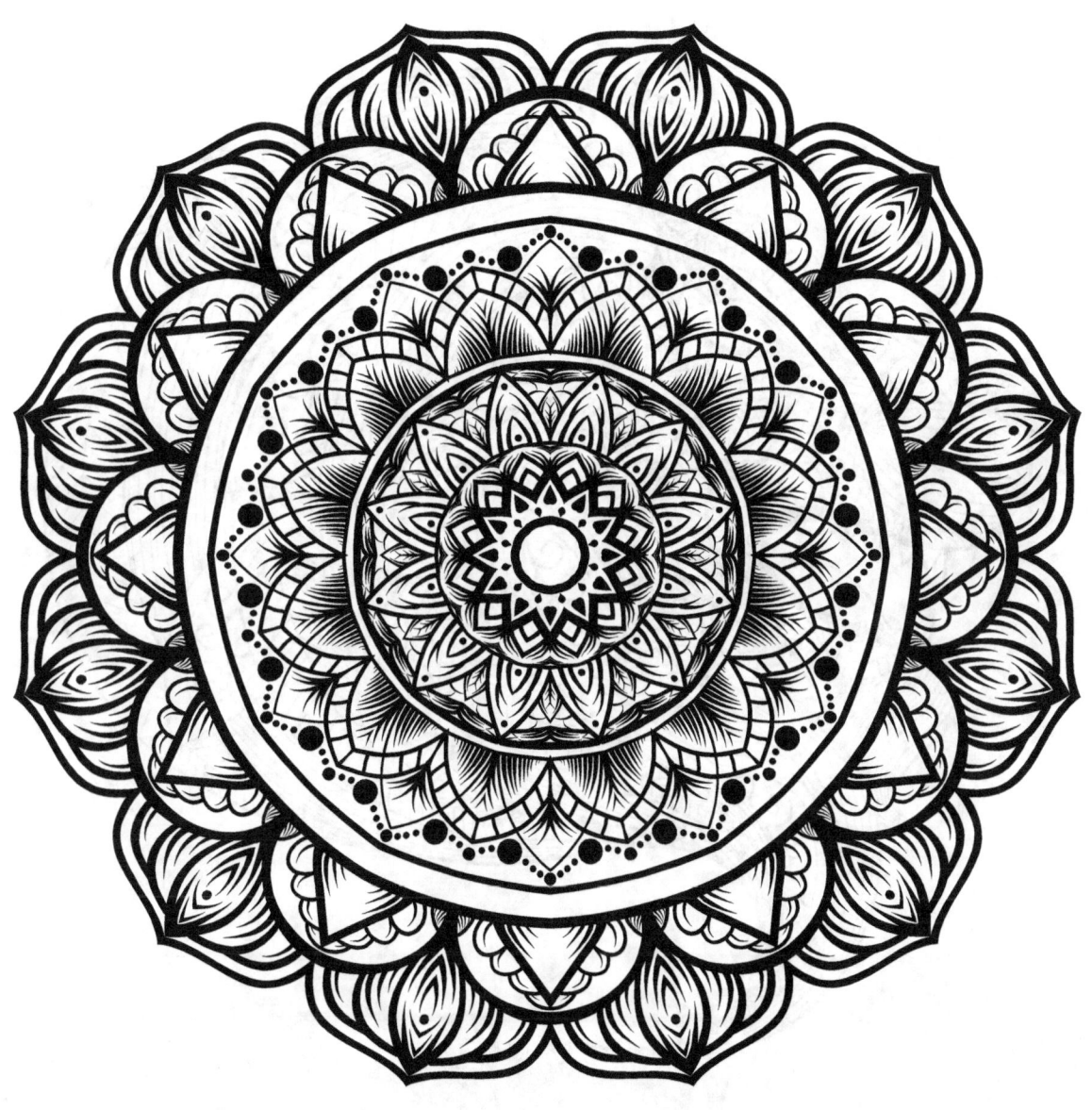

Choose the colors around your surroundings to fill this page.

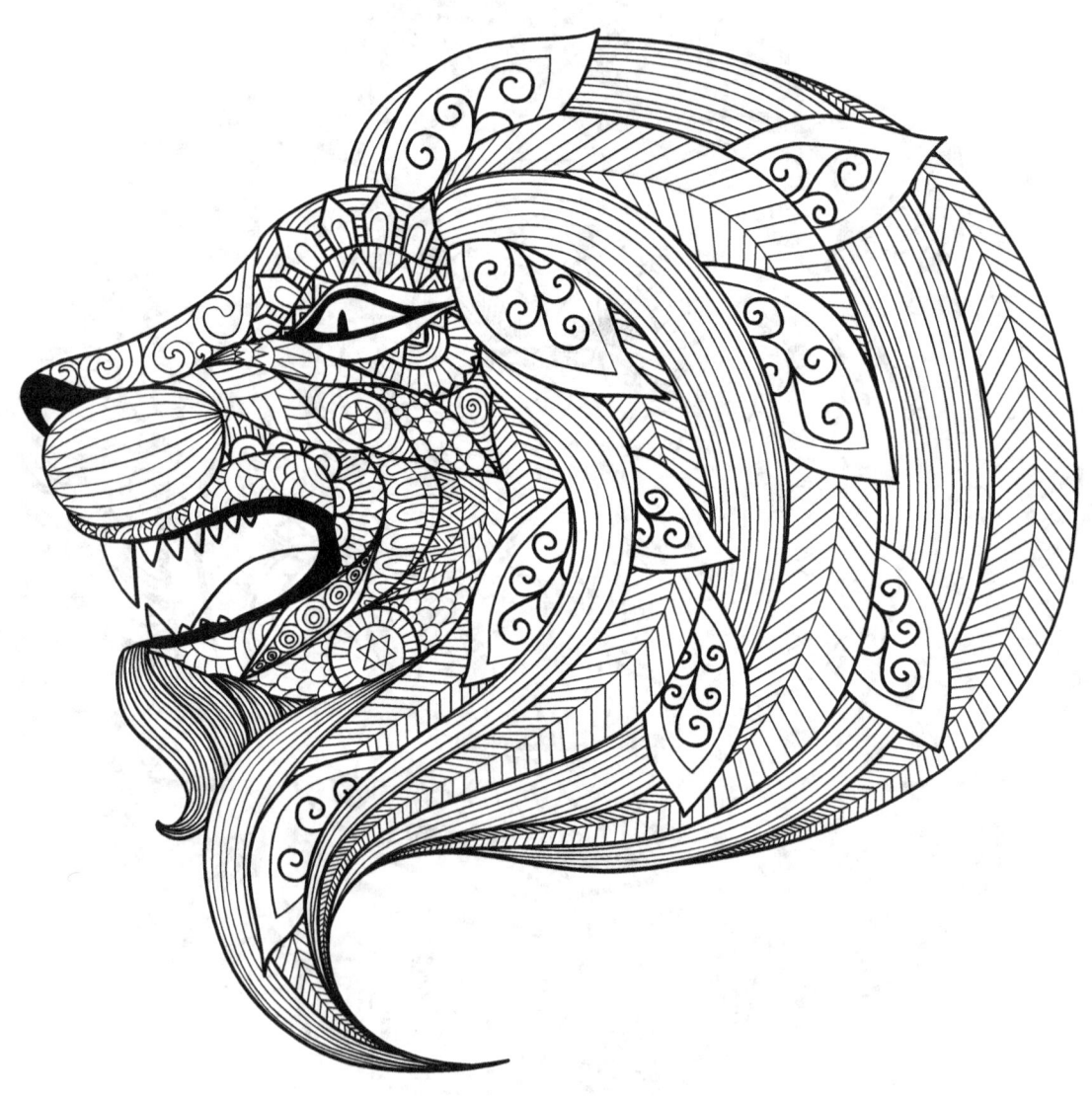

Imagine a forest in the midst of autumn. The leaves are changing colors, transforming into shades of gold, amber, and ruby.

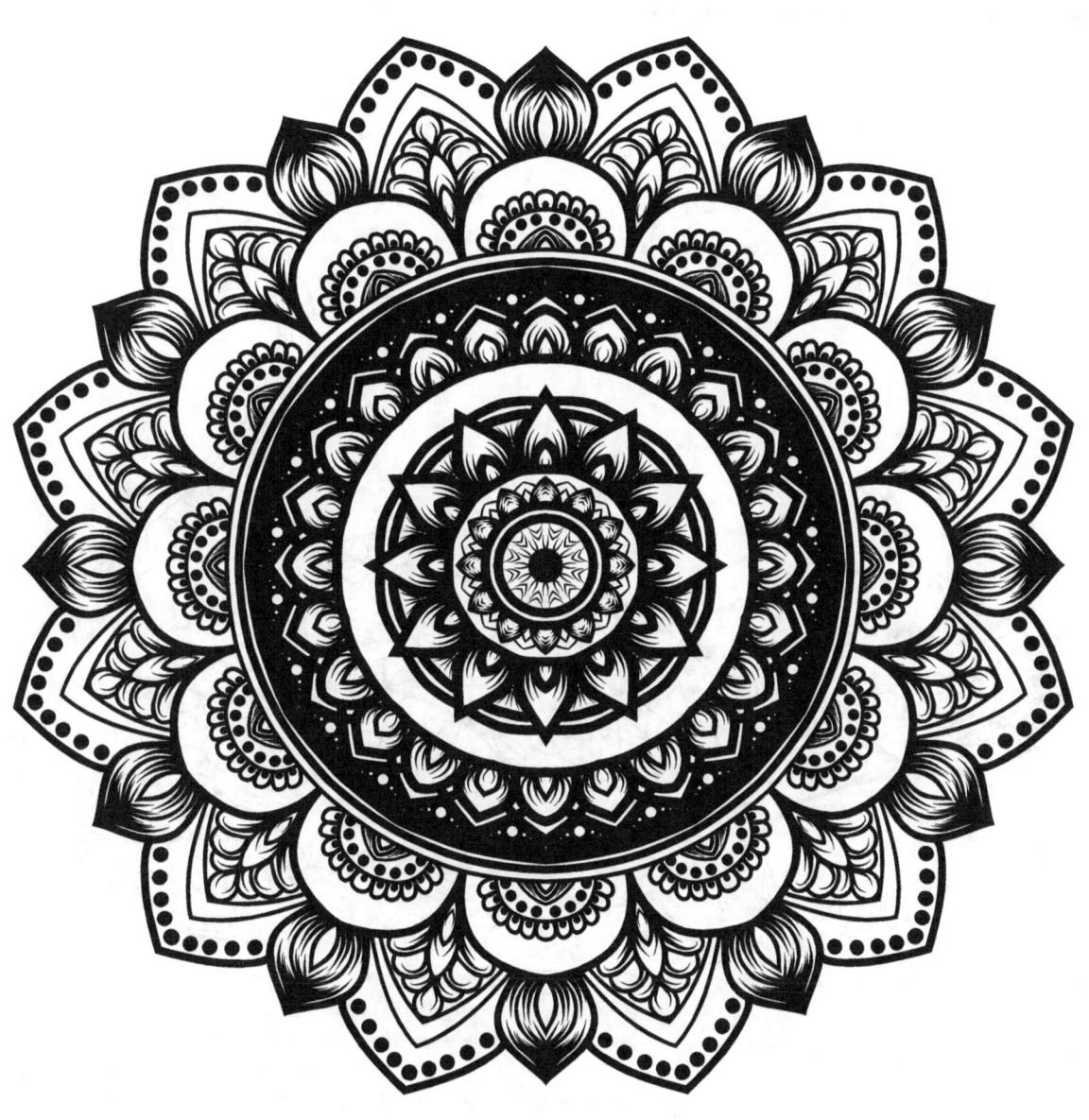

Pick a holiday theme and color here.

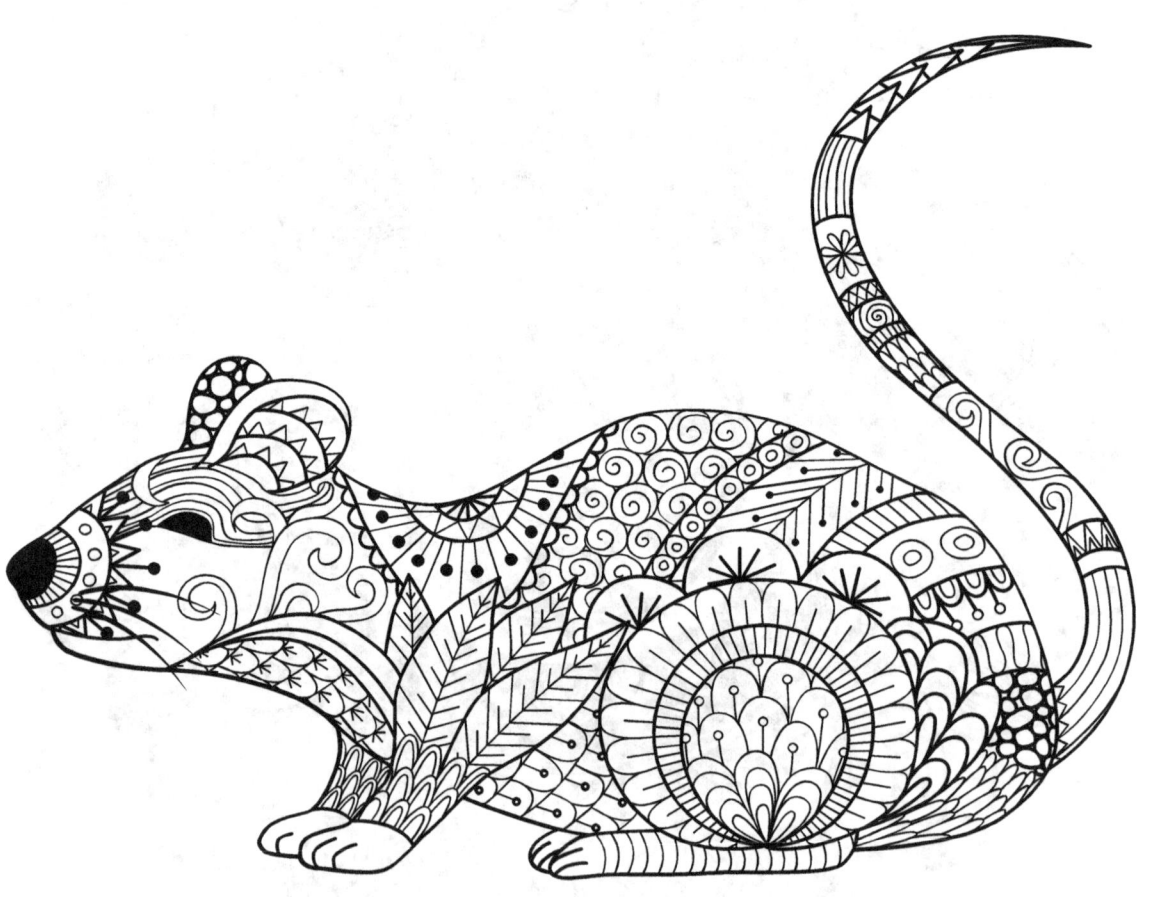

Go neutrals and browns with French vanilla palette.

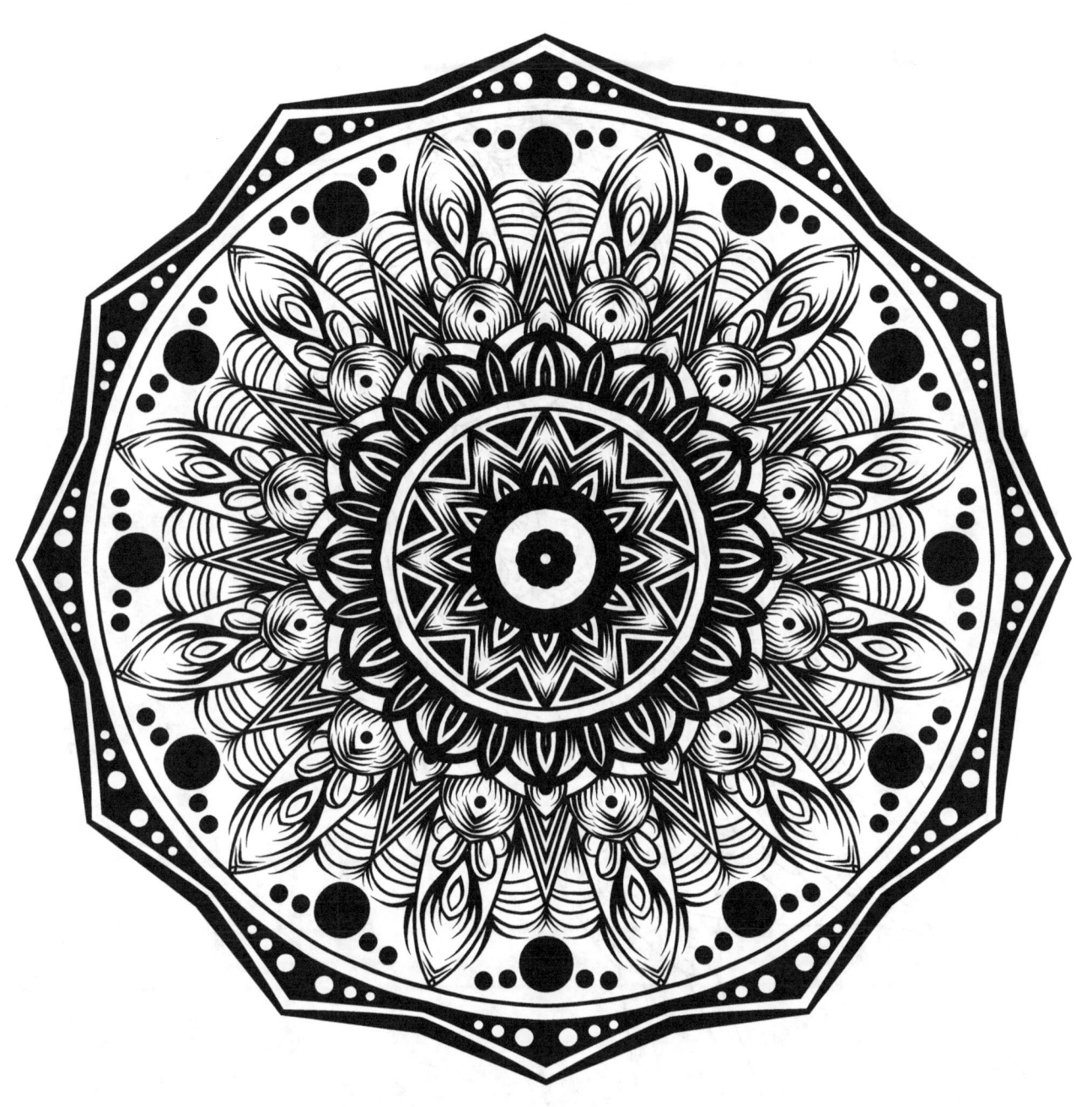

Paint with the colors of storm clouds. Various shades of dull blue, grey, black and white. Mix to make different shades.

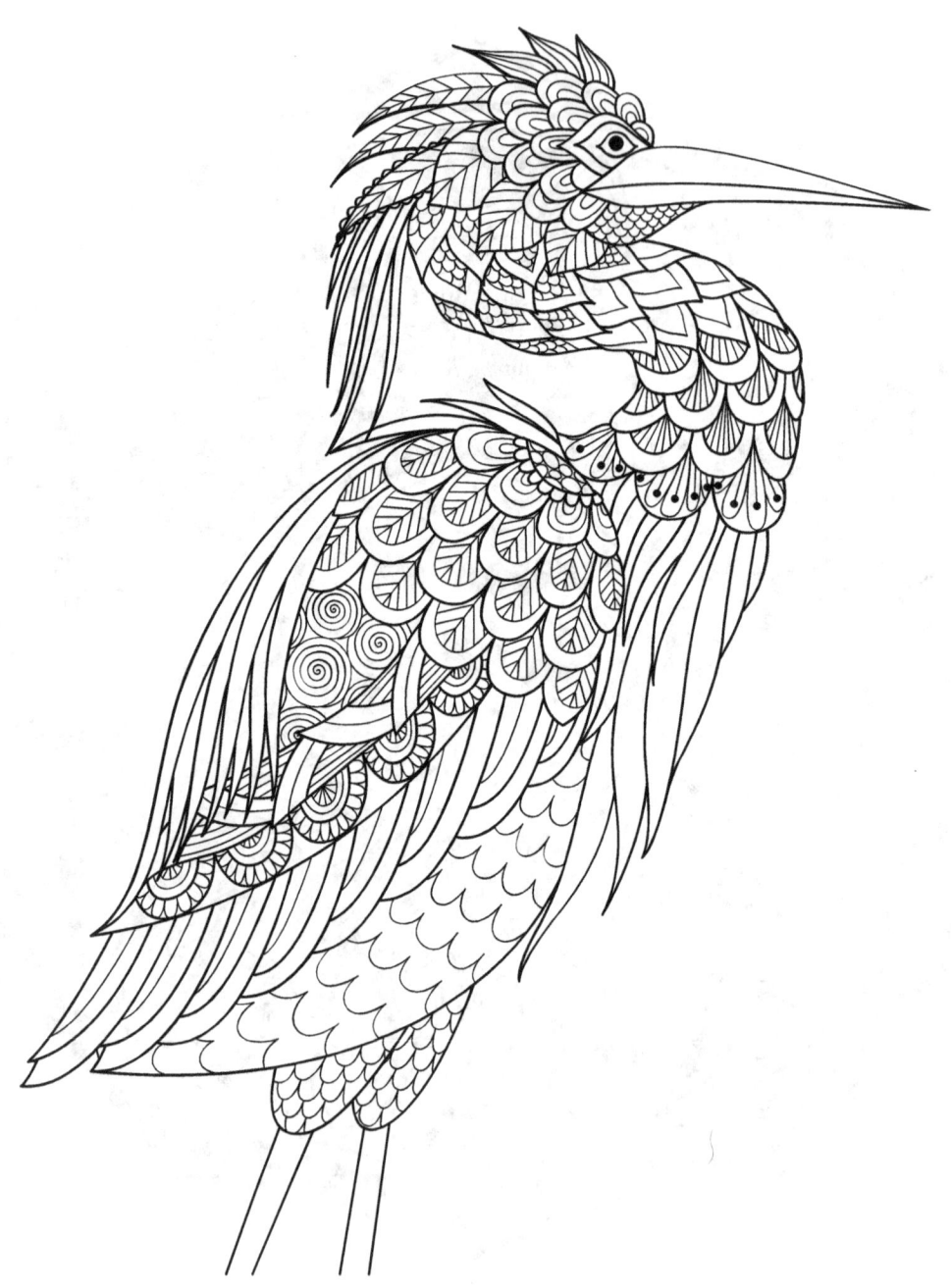

What colors do you see when you think of paradise?

Colors the earth fire water and air.

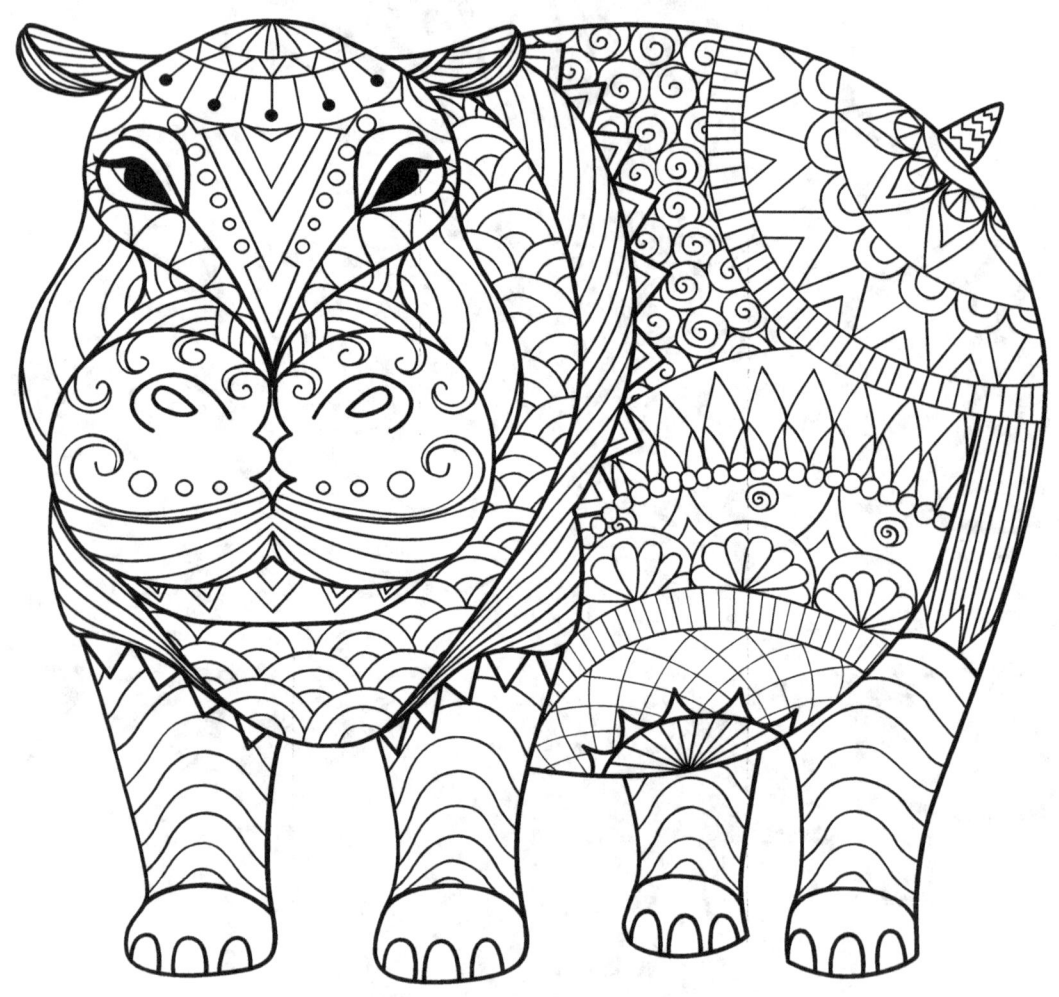

Fill in the colors of citrus punch.

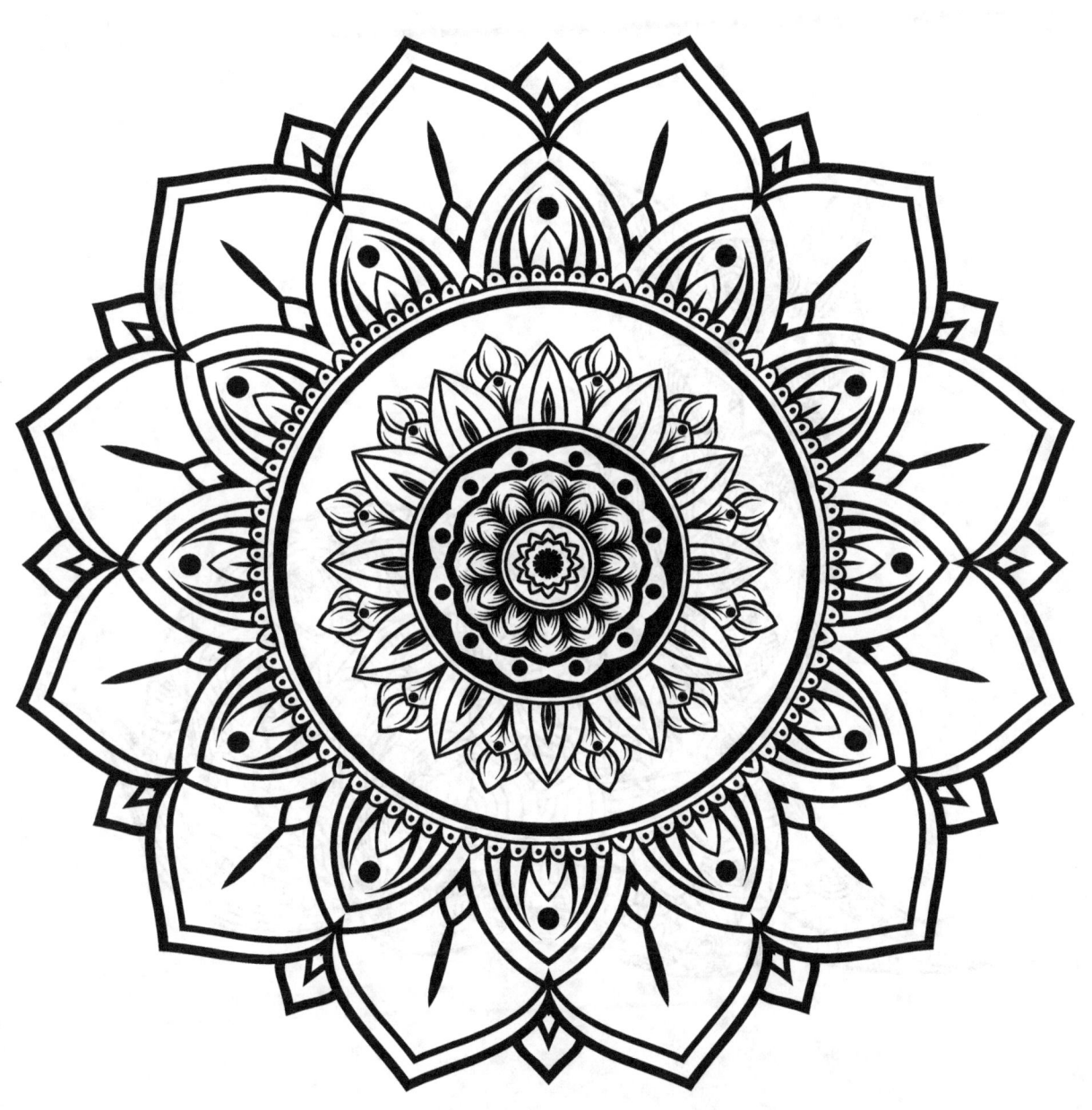

Choose a constellation that catches your eye and color it in with deep, rich colors that remind you of the mystery and wonder of the universe.

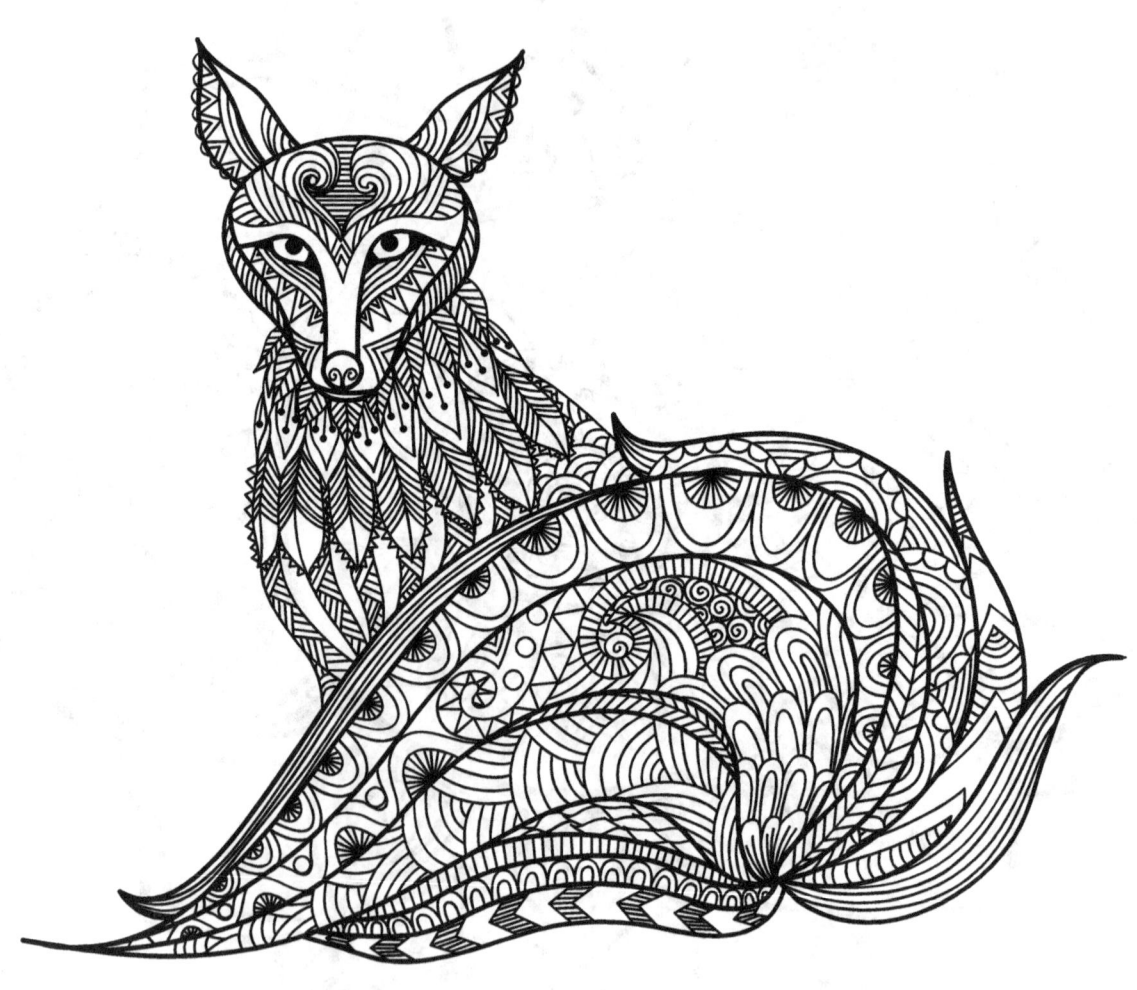

Think of beach towels. Colors that are fun in the sun and stand out !

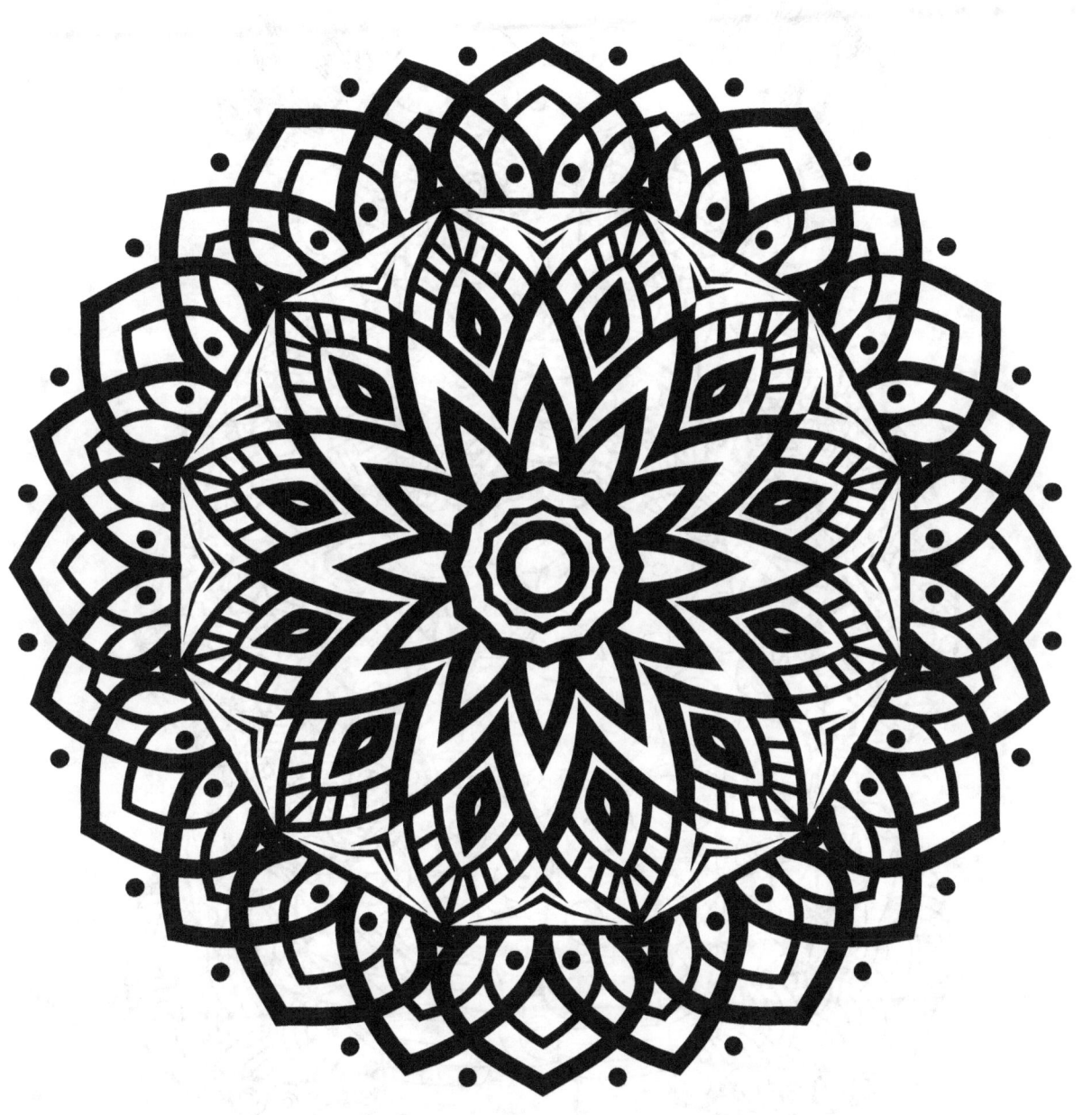

Paint it with the colors of roses, reds, pink, yellow and even black!

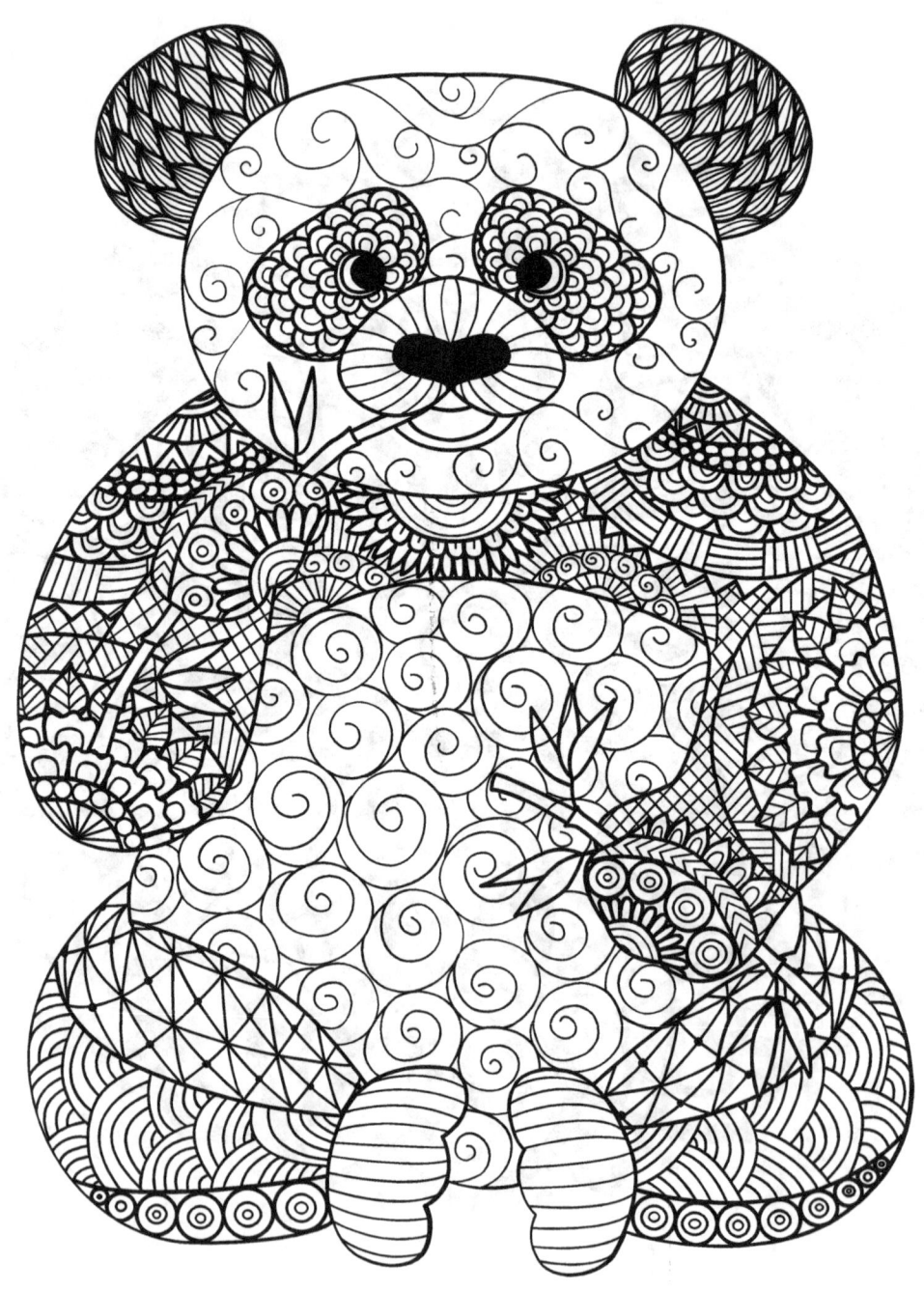

Fill it in with patterns. Checkered, Cheetah and zebra.

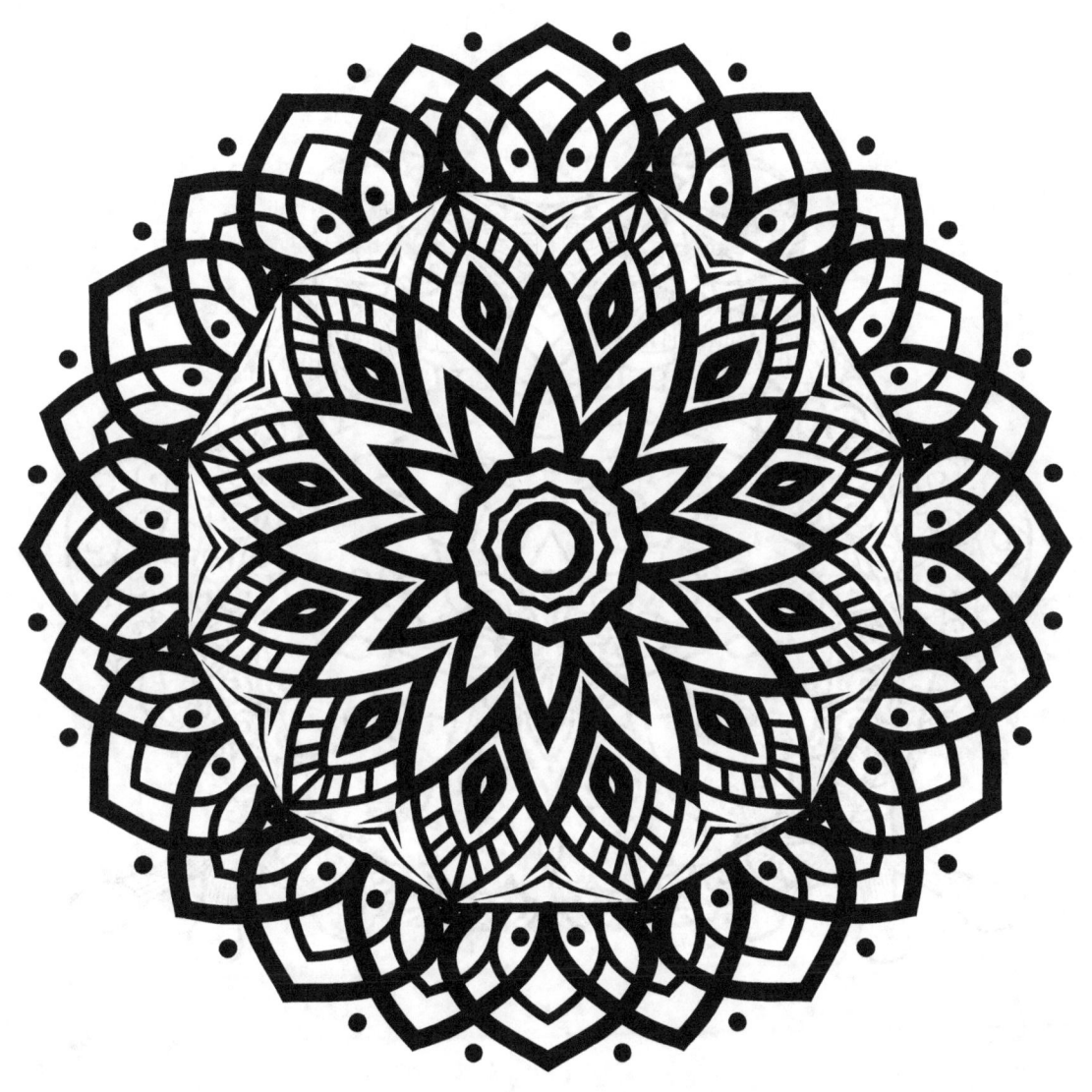

Pink 3 colors, and 3 prints from your wardrobe. Mix and match and color it here.

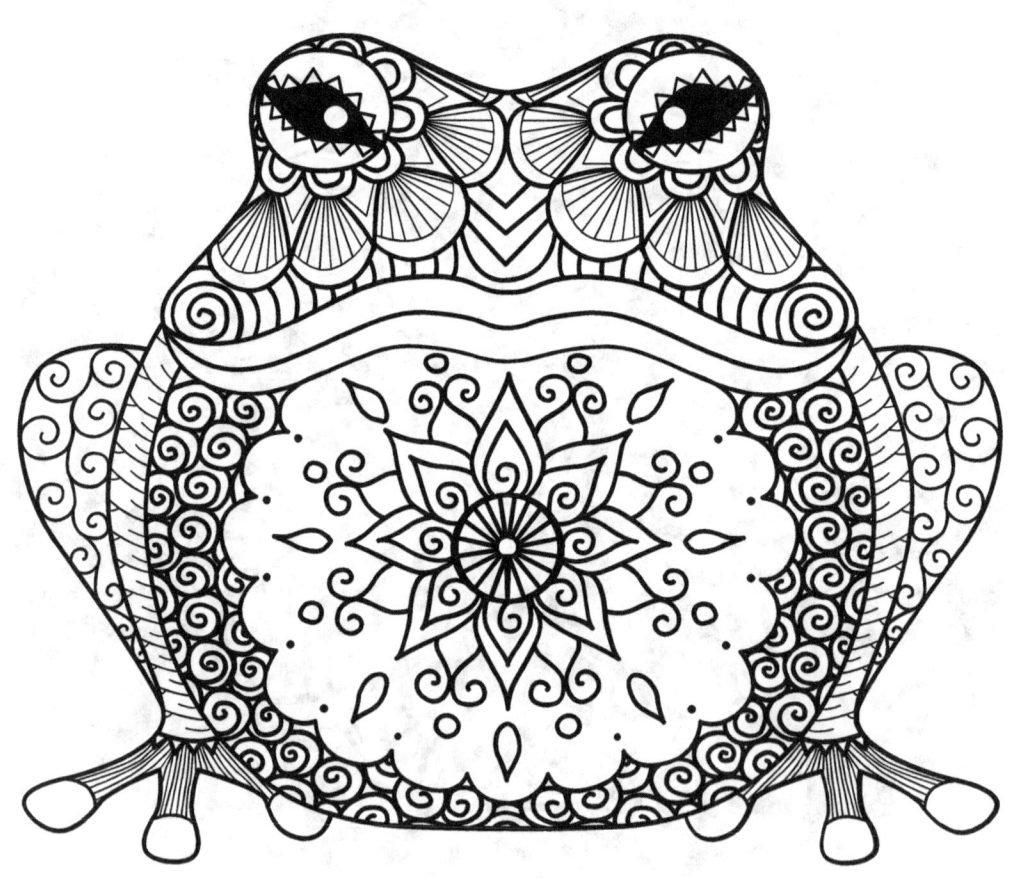

Color it with shades you'd find on mint chocolate chip.

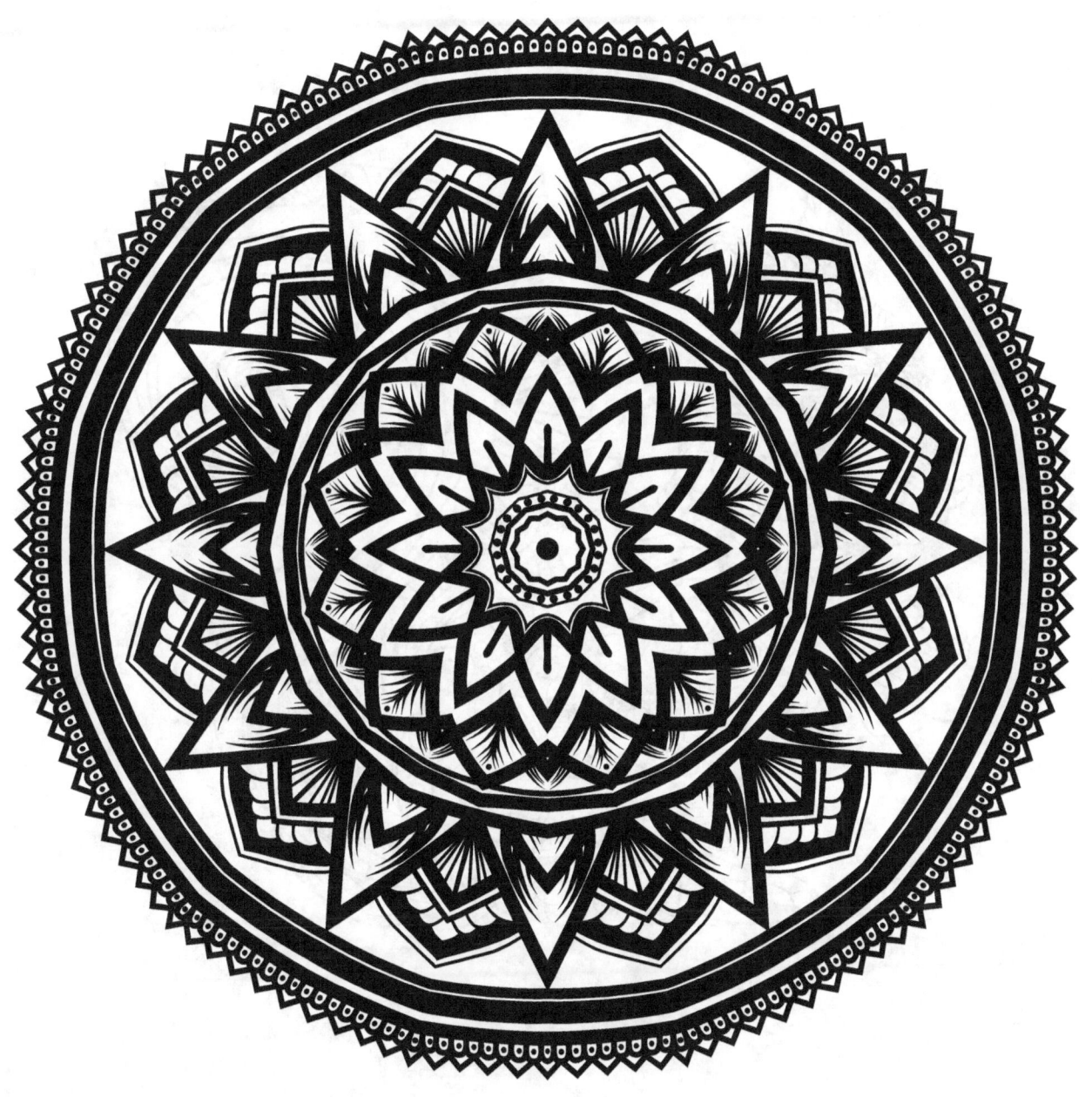

Close your eyes. Pick 4 colors randomly. Use those
colors in the mandala above

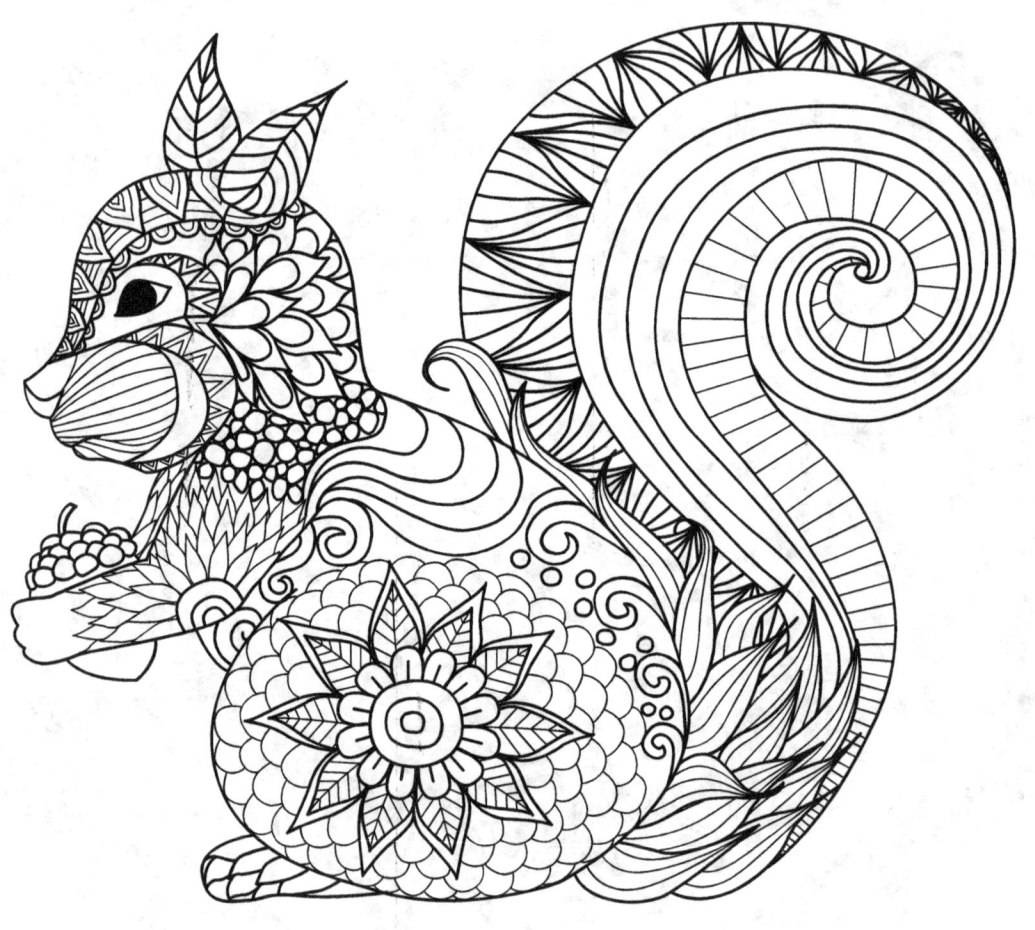

Think of a bouquet flowers. Daisies, daffodils, rose, tulips and poppy

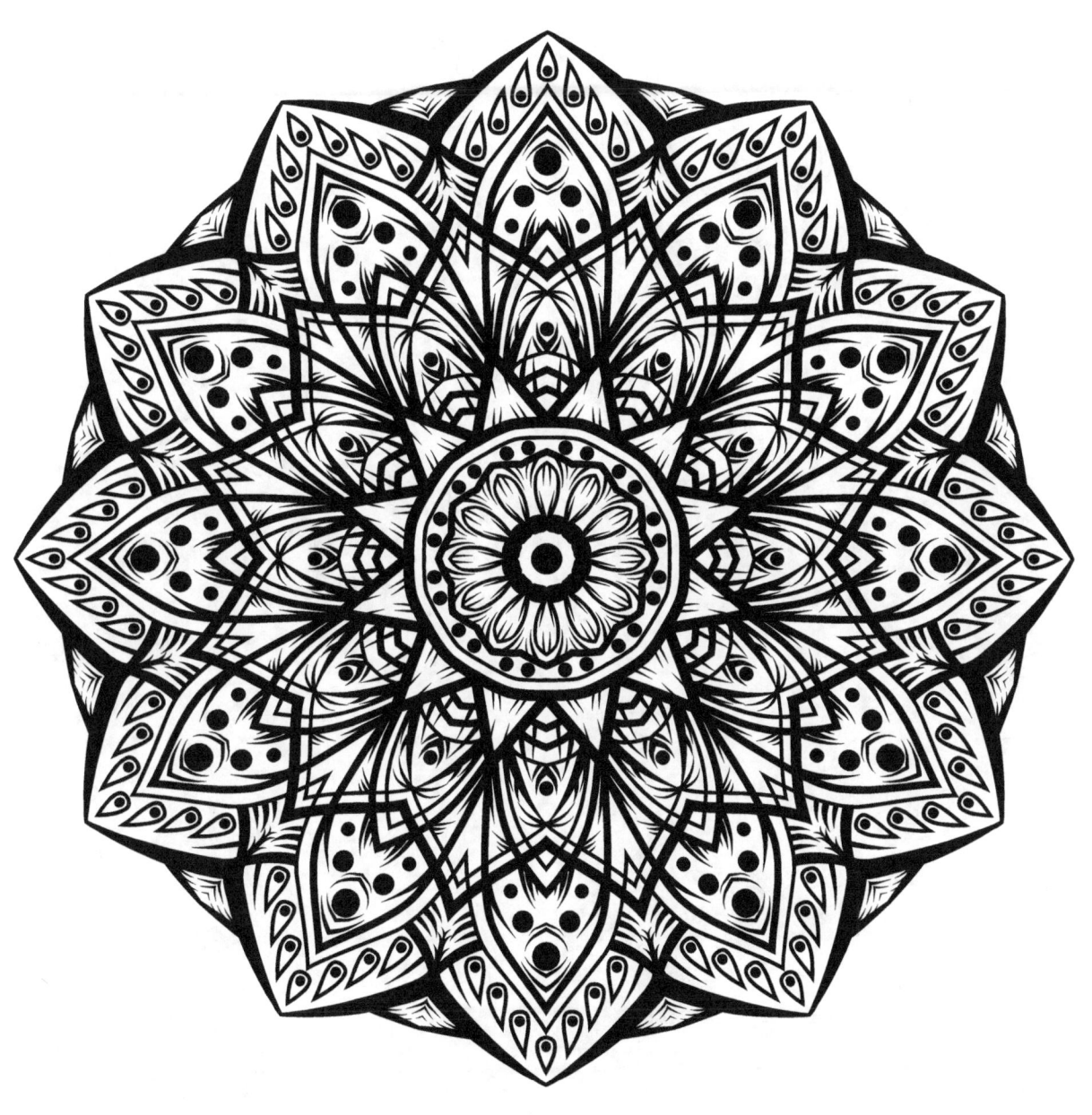

Fill this page with the colors of spring. From Warm greens, yellows, orange reds to peachy pinks.

Mix fire and ice.

Think of a winter dawn. Cool tones of blue with warm orange.

Think of your new home. What theme would you choose? Color it in.

Multicolor. Fill with every possible color you can.

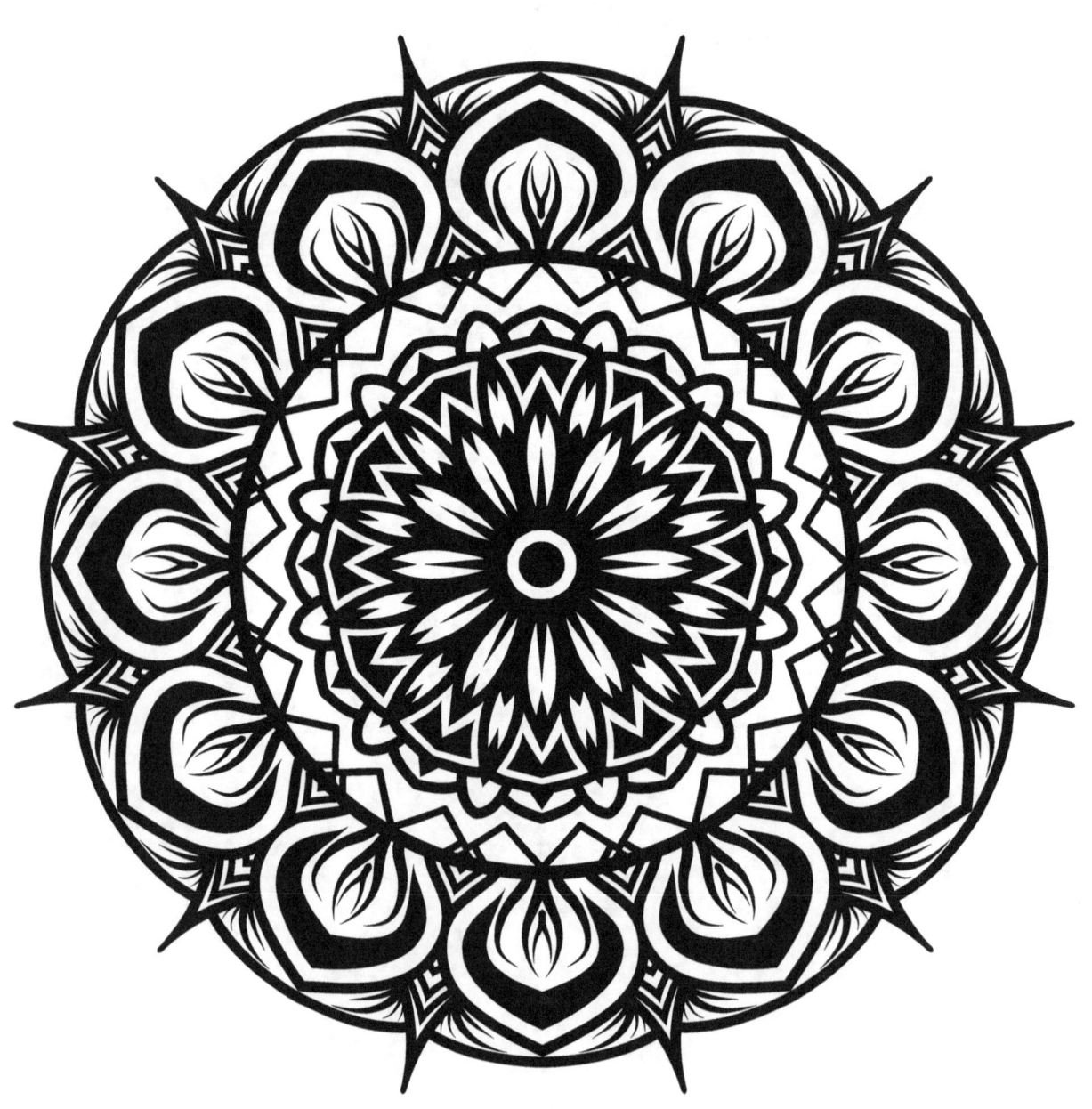

Fill it with hippie colors. Include purple, indigoes, violets and lilacs.

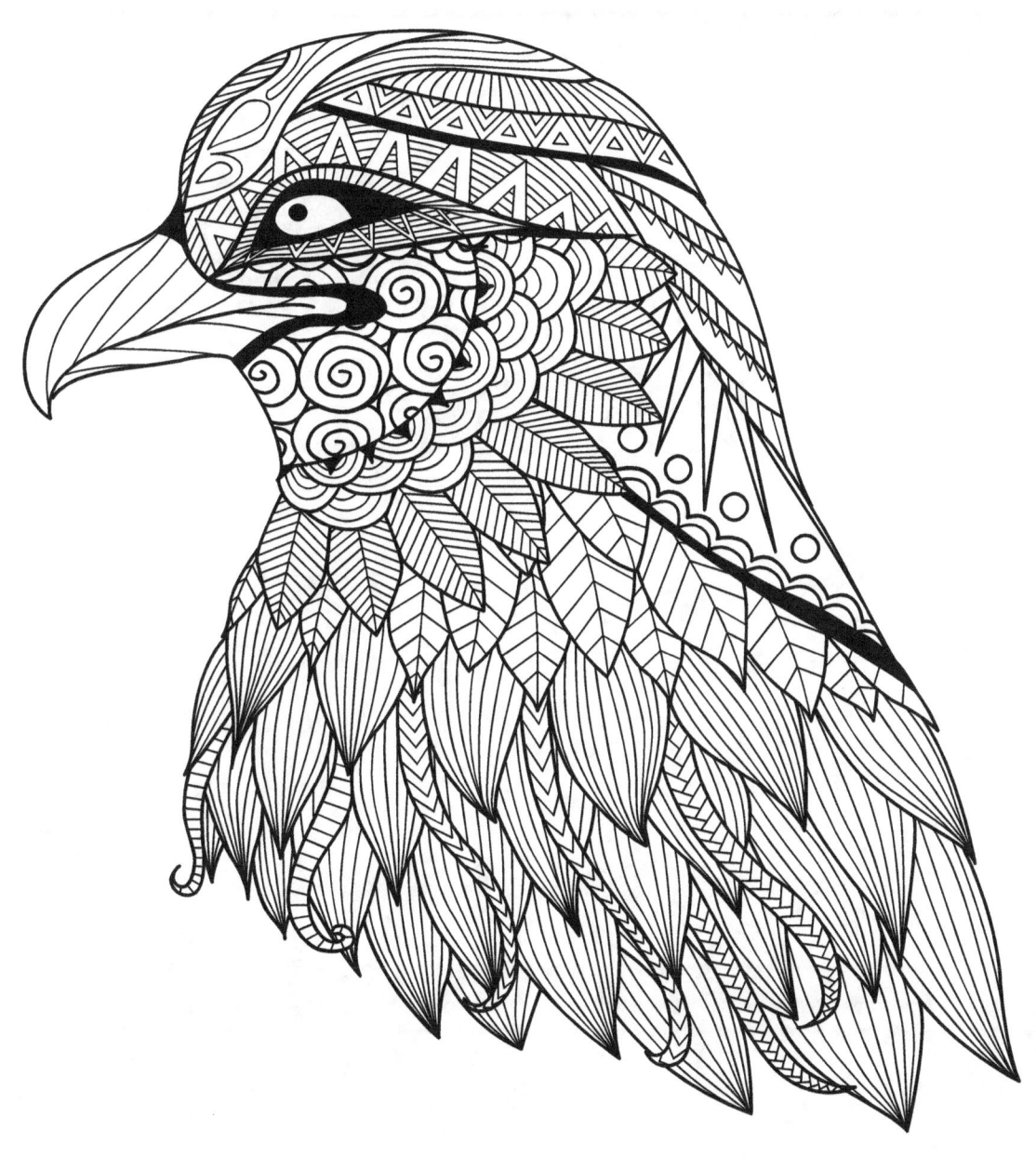

Color it with the choice of your favorite artist's piece.

Psychedelic include shrooms, Neon's and lots of vibrant color merging together.

Different shades of bubblegum.

Fill in blues. Mix in and create a variety. Cerulean blue, denim, stone blue, ice and indigo.

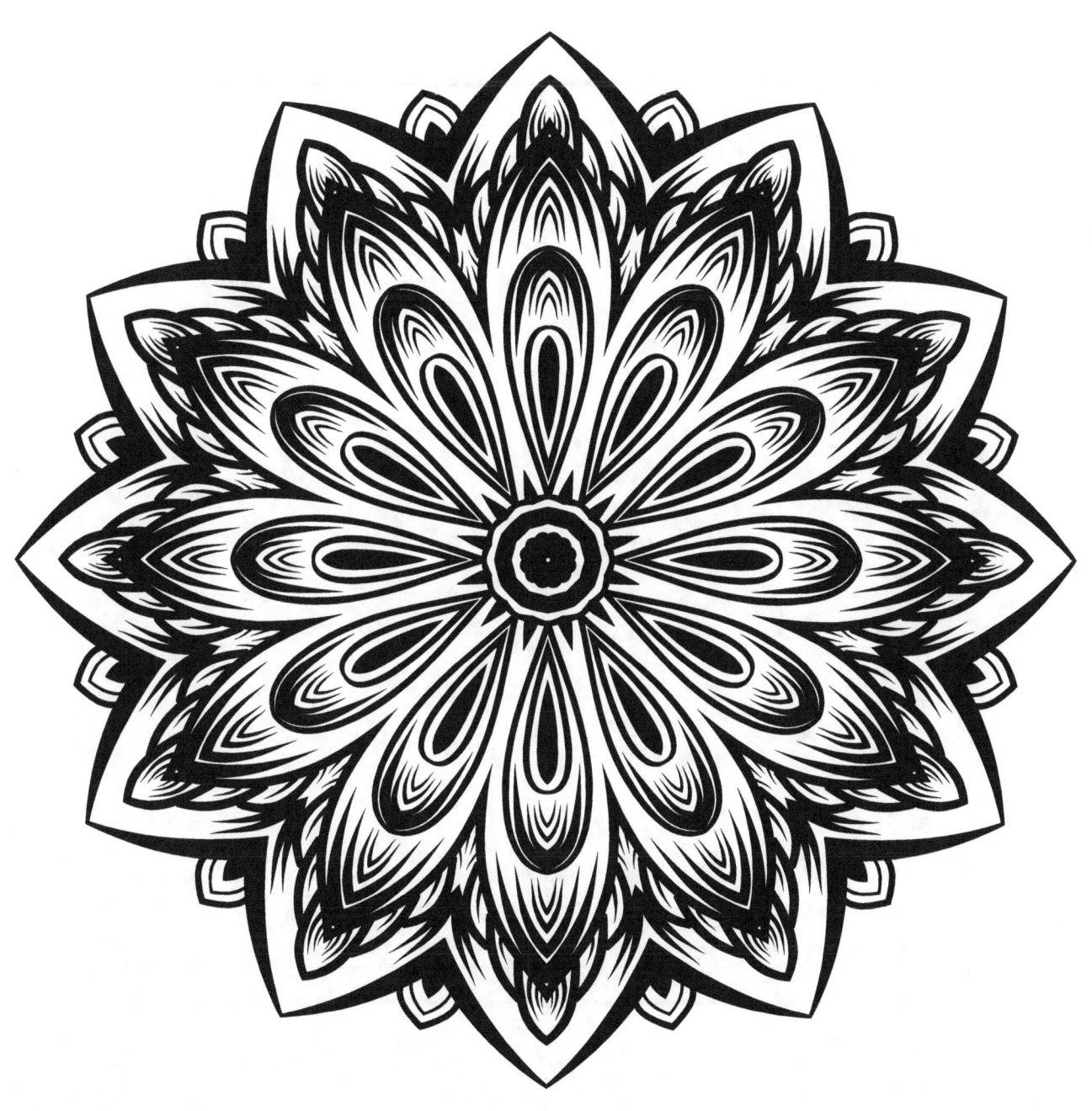

Reds comes in all shades. Pour your imagination with candy red, ruby red, cranberry red, wine, scarlet and mahogany.

Go free. Include a variety of colors that you like.

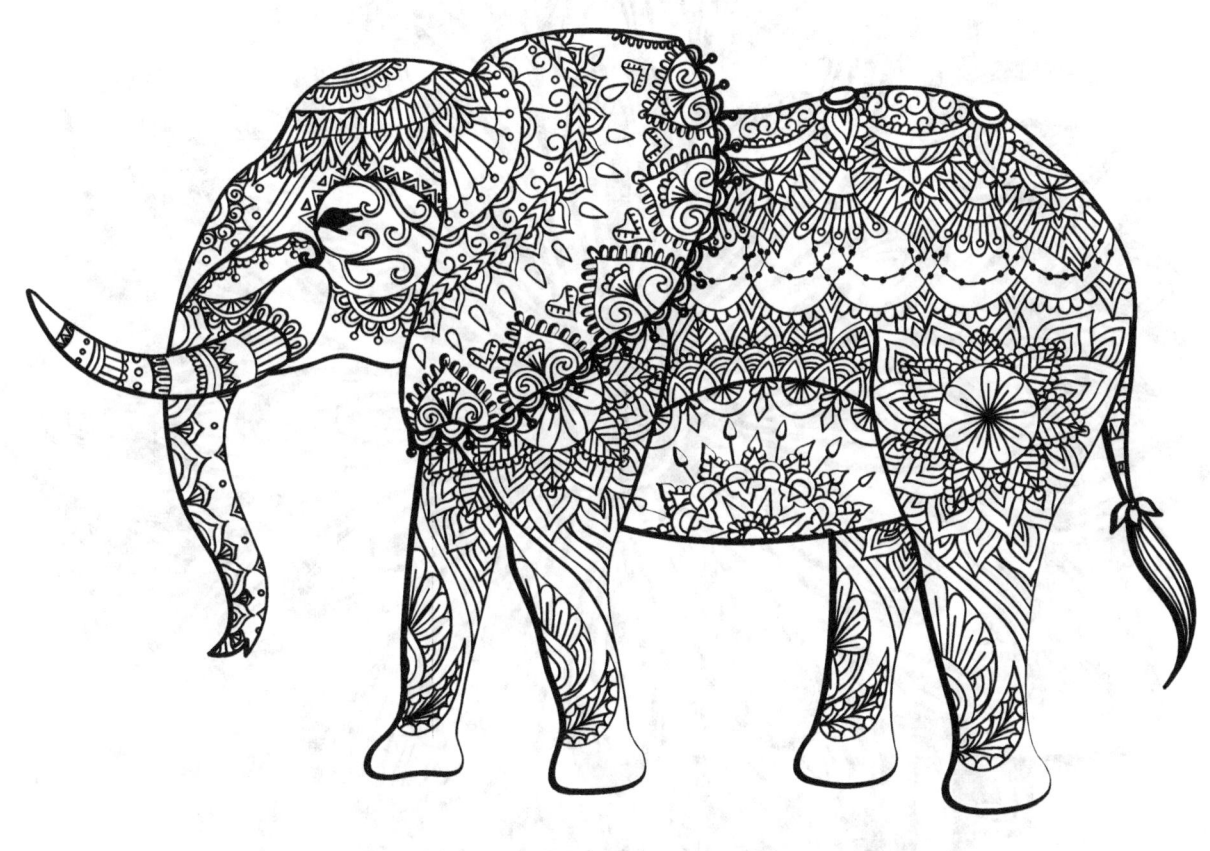

. Choose to go for an Atlantic palette. Add autumn leaves, red passion, Cardigan green and hazy skies grey.

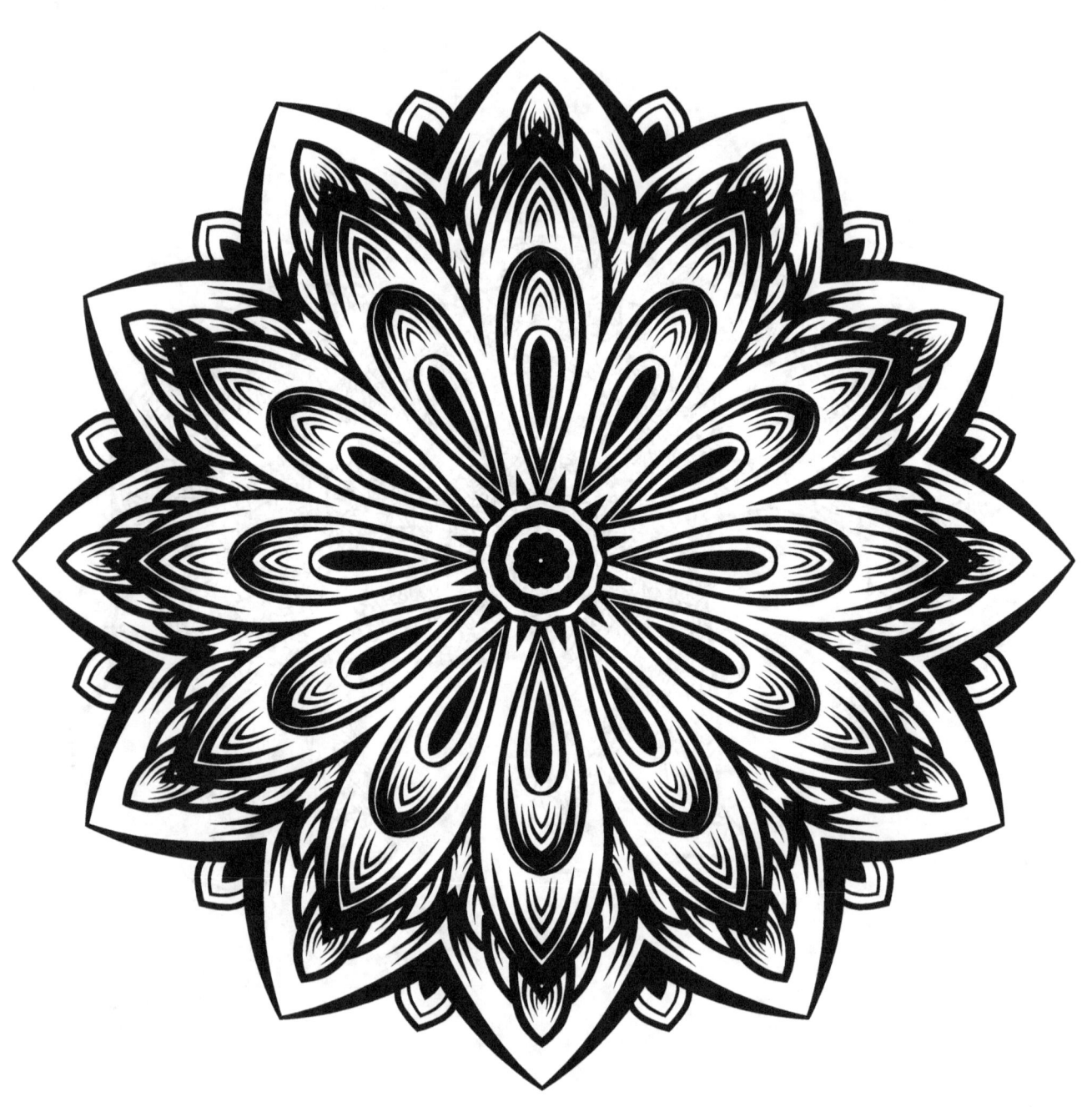

Think of yellow around you. Lemon yellow, honey, amber, pineapple and corn yellow.

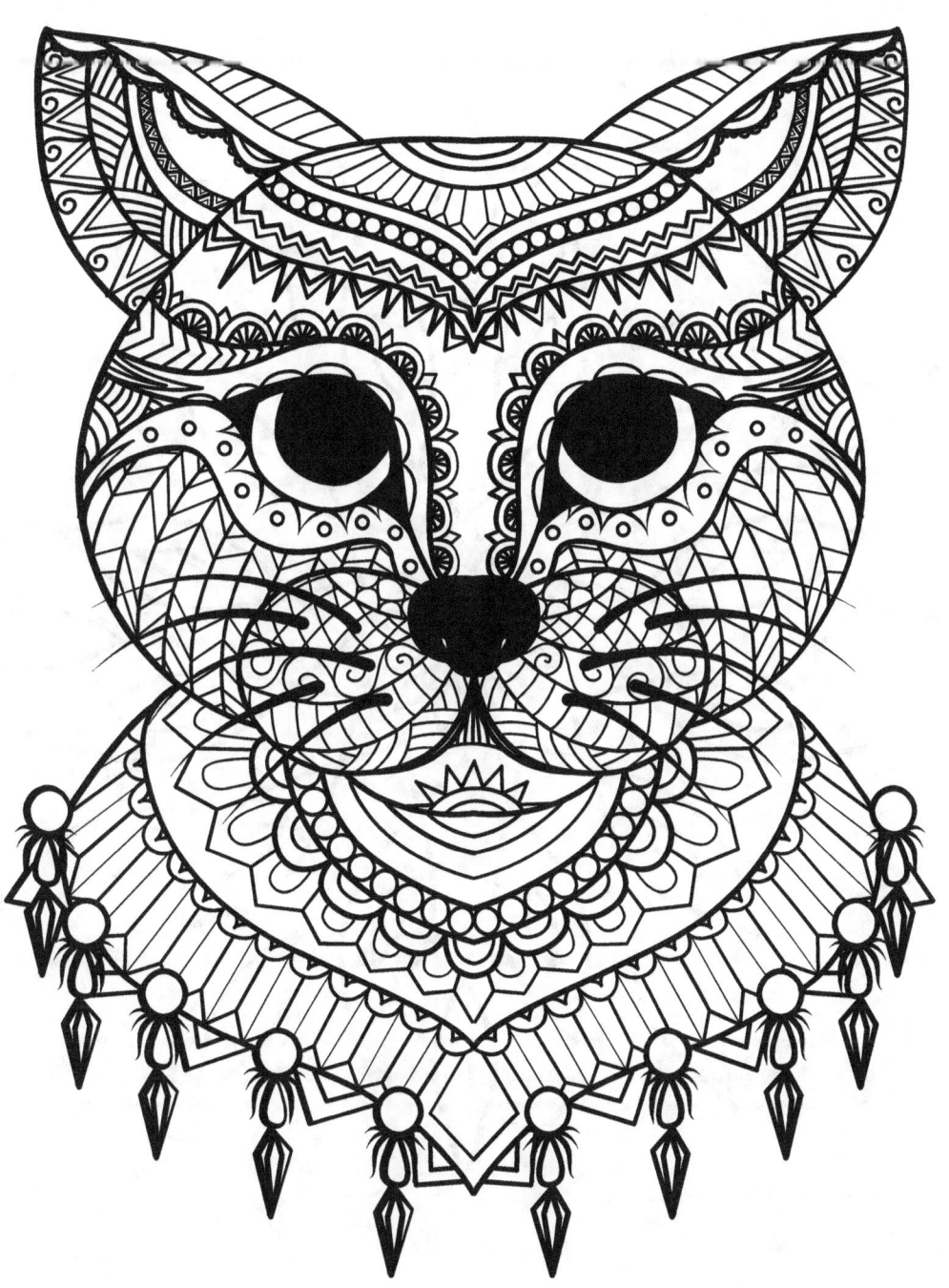

Color with a palette of a mythical creature that you can think of.

Colors of your favorite food.

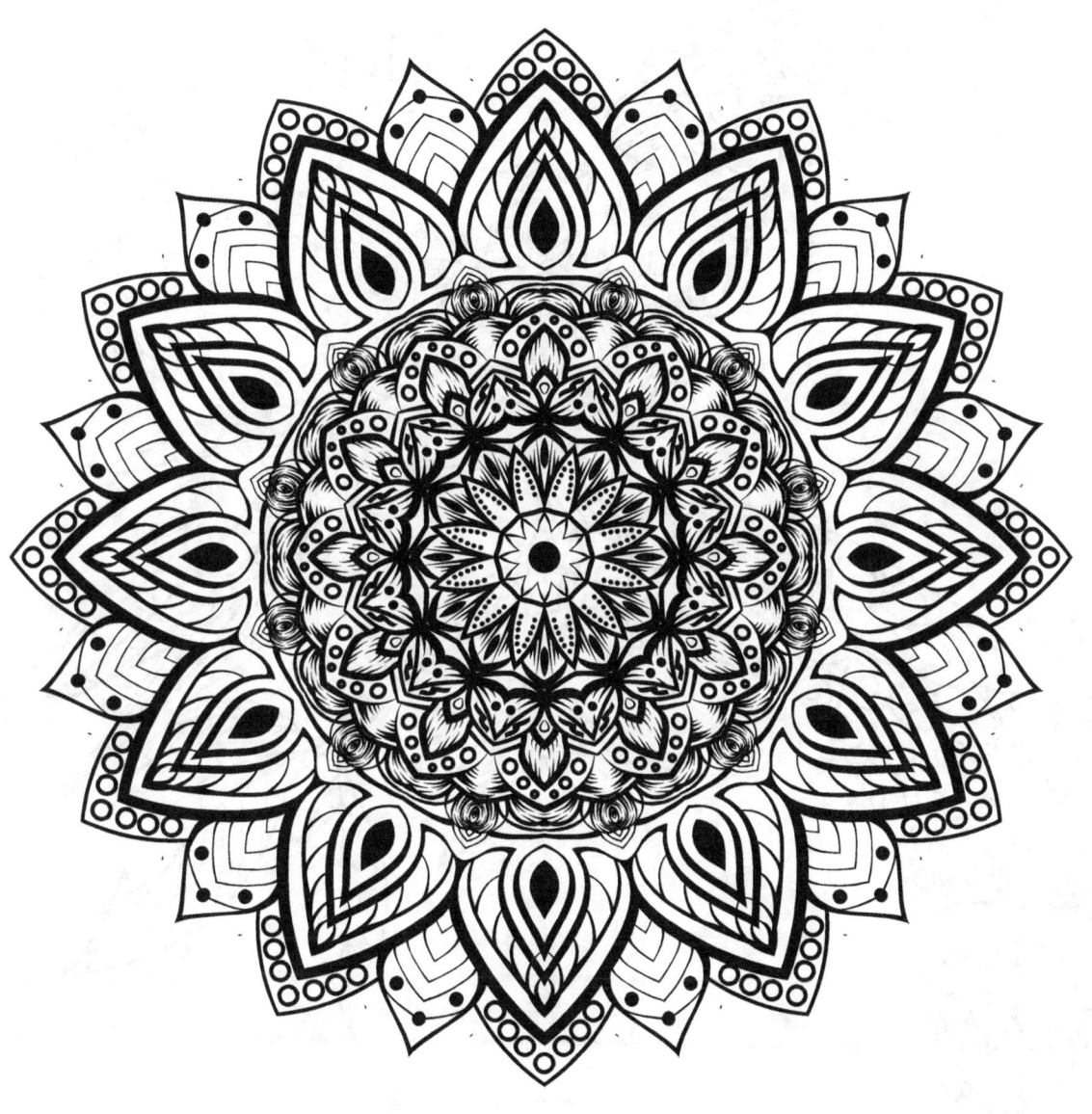

Fill in with baby colors. Calm, restful and nurturing.

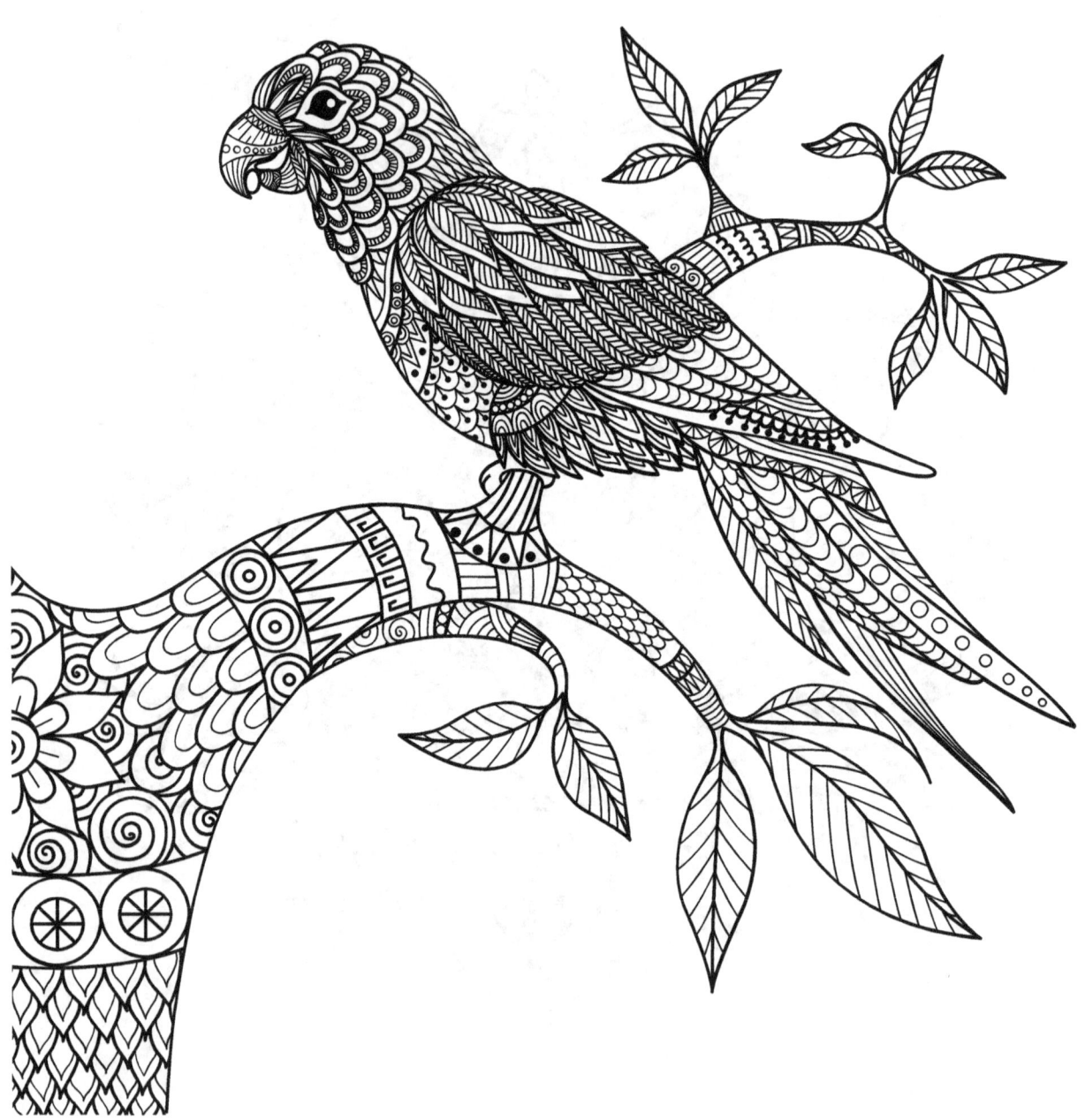

Synthwave: Cool, retro colors with a futuristic vibe.

www.ingramcontent.com/pod-product-compliance
Lightning Source LLC
Chambersburg PA
CBHW080844220526

45467CB00008B/2380